The Healing Stream

The Healing Stream

Catholic Insights into the
Ministry of Healing

GEORGE HACKER

DARTON · LONGMAN + TODD

First published in 1998 by
Darton, Longman and Todd Ltd
1 Spencer Court
140-142 Wandsworth High Street
London SW18 4JJ

ISBN 0–232–52249–9

A catalogue record for this book is available from the British Library.

Designed and produced by Sandie Boccacci
using QuarkXPress on an Apple PowerMac 7500
Set in 10/13.5pt Palatino
Printed and bound in Great Britain by
Redwood Books, Trowbridge, Wiltshire

Contents

Introduction

3RD WOMAN: Do tell me, Lazarus (with a nervous giggle) – I hope I'm not being impertinent – but what does it feel like to be dead?

2ND MAN: My dear! What a question to ask a man in the middle of dinner!

3RD WOMAN: Oh, but it's so important! Please! . . .

LAZARUS (as he speaks the conversation dies away into an inquisitive silence): This life is like weaving at the back of the loom. All you see is the crossing of the threads. In that life you go round to the front and see the wonder of the pattern.

3RD WOMAN: What sort of pattern is it?

LAZARUS: Beautiful and terrible. And – how can I tell you? – it is familiar . . .

(Dorothy Sayers, *The Man Born to be King*)[1]

'THIS LIFE IS LIKE weaving at the back of the loom. All you see is the crossing of the threads. In *that* life you go round to the front and see the wonder of the pattern.' Lazarus's answer to the tiresome woman at the supper table in Dorothy Sayers' *The Man Born to be King* sets the tone for any book on the ministry of healing. It is a subject which needs to be approached with humility and openness of mind and wonder. As we shall see again and again in this book healing is a very untidy subject. Yet when light does break through, and we catch a glimpse of the pattern, it can be awesome.

This untidiness was well illustrated for me by a programme I saw some years ago on TV about so-called 'miracle cures'. A number of people were interviewed who had had cancer and been given no hope of recovery by their doctors. The first woman described how deeply distressed she had been when she learned what was wrong with her, and how she had gone to her vicar for help. He, incredibly, had told her that her condition was a punishment for sin! Her reaction was to be so angry that she not only never went to church again, but became absolutely determined to get better to prove him wrong. And she did! She was followed by a couple, who described how their daughter had been suddenly struck down with a particularly pernicious form of leukemia. It was a complicated story of two fairly nominal churchgoers, who by a series of coincidences (which they now no longer saw as coincidences) had been led to Dorothy Kerin's Christian Healing Centre at Burrswood. There in the Church of Christ the Healer the girl had received the laying on of hands and anointing and had been instantly and totally healed.

I find stories like these both fascinating and challenging. But – as we shall discover if we have not already done so – that is what the ministry of healing is like. On the one hand it poses near insoluble questions. Why should one person be healed and not another? What part does faith play? What about non-Christian healings? On the other it challenges us to a whole new way of looking at life – to a world where the unexpected happens, where attitudes of mind can have dramatic effects on our physical wellbeing, and where expectations over such things as prayer are greatly enlarged. At the same time it invites us to explore the deepest theological questions – God's purpose for his creation, the nature of evil, his way of salvation – and to come at them in the most practical way through - individuals that we know, who, with us, have to make sense of the pain that has invaded their lives. Equally it warns us against easy answers and theories – again by way of the practical, because our lightest word can have the most profound effect on someone struggling to come to terms with the suffering that has struck them. It is indeed a tangle of threads, like the back of Lazarus's loom – but a fascinating and challenging tangle!

This is an exciting time to write about healing. Books on healing of course abound, as a glance at any church book-stall will tell you. Many of these are of the 'how I was healed' variety, but excitingly we are now beginning to get quite a number which get beneath this to some serious theological thinking. We are now well into the 'second generation' of the healing explosion of the past few decades, and that is usually the point with any movement when the really deep and impor-tant questions get asked.

The purpose of this book is to contribute to this discus-sion. With the Charismatic Movement occupying the high ground in the healing scene at the moment, there is a dearth of material on healing from the Catholic viewpoint and a real need to recover Catholic emphases and insights. This book is an attempt to fill that gap. However, having said that, the thing that always impresses me about the ministry of healing is the way in which it simply refuses to be taken over by any one theological approach – Catholic or otherwise. It always makes the running. And the reason it does so is because it deals all the time with 'real' experiences. Sickness is real, pain is real, and so is recovery when it happens. And that inevitably means coming up against uncomfortable facts which won't be fitted into neat theological schemes. So Liberals, for example, find themselves having to make room for the miraculous, Catholics for the eruption of ministerial grace outside the confines of holy order, Evangelicals for the acceptance of traditional bogeymen like prayers for the dead, and Charismatics for powerlessness and failure. In the end 'healing' as it is experienced in reality, simply won't allow itself to be owned by any one theological tradition. Once again we are back to Lazarus's tangle of threads.

The word 'Catholic' needs explaining. 'Do you mean "Catholic" with a small "c" or a big one?' people have asked me when I have told them what I am writing about. The answer to that question is to be found in the first chapter, where I have tried to set out what I understand by the word 'Catholic'. Not everyone will agree with my somewhat impressionistic picture.

A Roman Catholic would have written differently, I am sure, as would a traditional Anglo-Catholic in the Church of England. I suspect too that some of my more 'Liberal' friends in the Affirming Catholicism Movement, of which I am a member, would have reservations about some of the things in this book. But having said that, I do believe that there are certain insights and emphases that can truly be termed 'Catholic' and which transcend any differences that there are. It is these that are important to our understanding of the ministry of healing, and it is these that this book is mainly about.

As so often happens finding a suitable title was one of the hardest tasks. In the end we settled for *The Healing Stream* – largely because it conveys the sense of being carried along by something bigger than yourself, which is very much of the essence of what it means to be a Catholic. Also it suggests something which has flowed down through the centuries. I had hoped to find a direct quotation to fit the title, but there was nothing that exactly matched it. The words from the well-known hymn,

> Open now the crystal fountain
> Whence the healing stream doth flow ...[2]

perhaps came nearest to what I was looking for, but the reference there is really to healing grace rather than to the Church. However the two are closely connected, and the Church is nothing if the healing grace of Christ does not flow through it. Certainly the Scripture passage on which these lines are based has never been far from my mind:

Then the angel showed me the river of the water of life, sparkling like crystal, flowing from the throne of God and of the Lamb ... On either side of the river stood a tree of life, which yields twelve crops of fruit, one for each month of the year. The leaves of the trees are for the healing of the nations.[3]

Finally I have to say that writing this book has been something of a spiritual pilgrimage for me, and I am very conscious of the way that my life has been touched through it. I suspect that often happens to people who are given a major task to accomplish, but when the subject is such an exciting and challenging one as the ministry of healing, then it is almost certain to be so. For that I am deeply grateful, as also for those who in their different ways have encouraged me – by their writings, by the way they have shared their knowledge and experiences with me, by their patience and support, and by their prayers.

GEORGE HACKER
December 1997

1 A Rich and Varied Pattern

An overview of Catholic insights in general

'Whatever meaning people bring to Catholicism, it does represent a multi-layered theological, ecclesiastical and social mosaic which is of great importance to the Church.'

(The Archbishop of Canterbury at the Affirming Catholicism Conference at York 1991)[1]

YOU CANNOT WRITE a book on the 'Catholic' approach to healing without first asking what is the 'Catholic' approach to life in general. For me it was a self-professed agnostic, the actor and director Jonathan Miller, who provided the most vivid answer to that question, in a brief but unforgettable 'still' from his past. Interviewed by Gerald Priestland in the radio programme *The Case Against God*, Jonathan Miller said:

I can remember the only time ... that I have ever been moved to tears by something which was not a direct emotional incident in my own life, quite unexpectedly in public, was [when I was] walking with my wife through the aisle of St Anthony's Cathedral in Padua about lunchtime, and I was passing by one of the side chapels, and there was a man in a raincoat, I think his hand still gripping his briefcase. He was kneeling on the altar step receiving the sacrament. And the spectacle of this man reaching forward, his tongue poked forward, still with his hand gripping his briefcase, representing his day which had been briefly set aside and which was to be resumed a few moments later, taking his soul seriously – it moved me, and it moves me now to think of it.[2]

For me this brief snapshot captures much of the essential feel behind the word 'Catholic' as I understand it. There is the down-to-earthness of it – nipping into the cathedral for a spiritual 'top-up' during the lunch hour! There is the sense of the sacred being right there in the midst of ordinary life – the hand on the briefcase, the mouth open to receive the holy food. There is the unselfconsciousness of it – kneeling there in full view of passers-by, but knowing that you belong there, that you are part of something much bigger than yourself, much bigger than them, whatever they may think. There is the power of the ritual – nothing is said, nothing needs to be said; the action of giving and receiving, of feeding, says it all. And there is the sense of the awesomeness of it – that somehow a door has been opened and the Holy One is there, reaching out to touch and to bless.

The trouble, of course, with a word like 'Catholic' is that it embraces so many different thoughts and feelings. I like Archbishop George Carey's picture of a *mosaic*, a rich and varied pattern of colours and shapes. That is to approach the subject impressionistically, which has the advantage of not limiting the discussion to theology and abstract ideas. We will of course need in this first chapter to examine the theological insights and key ideas which lie behind the Catholic tradition, but we will also look at other bits of the mosaic as well, all of which contribute to the overall pattern – Church practices, ways of looking at life, the feel of what it means to be a 'Catholic'.

To start with theology, it has been said that of the different traditions, Catholics tend to focus on the *incarnation*, Liberals on the *ministry of Jesus*, Evangelicals on *the cross*, Orthodox on the *resurrection* and Charismatics on *Pentecost*. This is of course a simplification, but it does provide a clue to many of the differences that exist between them. Certainly *'incarnational'* is a keyword in Catholic theology, as we shall see again and again in this book. What it means is that Catholics view life against the background of belief in a Lord who is still deeply immersed in his world, and working for its salvation and healing. Especially he is seen as working through his 'body' the Church and through its sacraments – though not exclusively. So Catholics can speak of the Church as an 'extension' of the incarnation – the living Christ continuing his ministry among us through the 'channels' that he has chosen for this purpose. A key text in all this is the one from St John at the end of the Christmas Gospel: 'And the Word was made flesh, and dwelt among us, and we beheld his glory'.[3] Significantly this used to be read at the conclusion of every Eucharist with the implication that in the Eucharist he is still to be found dwelling among us and that we can know him and glimpse something of that glory. The poet, John Betjeman, exactly catches the feel of this in his well-known Christmas poem:

> No love that in a family dwells,
> No carolling in frosty air,
> Nor all the steeple-shaking bells
> Can with this single Truth compare -
> That God was Man in Palestine
> And lives today in Bread and Wine.[4]

This incarnational approach affects the outlook of Catholics in all sorts of ways, and is never far from the surface – as we shall come to recognize before we get very far into our study of the ministry of healing. At this point, however, we need only mention one aspect of it, but it is a very basic aspect – and that is the way it affects (or ought to affect) our view of matter. Esther de Waal recalls a conversation she once had with Lord George MacCleod as they walked round the cloisters of Iona Abbey. 'Everyone today keeps asking, "what is the matter?"', he said, 'and the short answer is MATTER is the matter. It is our view of matter, the extent to which the Church has spiritualized the faith and set it apart from the material world, that has brought us where we are today.'[5] Catholics have been as guilty of this as any, especially in their attitude to sex.

St Augustine has a lot to answer for here, with his teaching that sex was basically bad because it involved loss of control of the mind over the body (though it could be tolerated for the purpose of procreation!). He had enormous influence over the Western Church, and it is perhaps only in this century that Christians have begun to question this attitude to any marked degree. Yet there has always been a counter tradition, breaking out from time to time in individuals like the medieval mystic, Mother Julian of Norwich, and in the commonly held assumption that Catholics somehow manage to enjoy themselves rather more than Protestants! This latter perhaps owes more to culture than theology, but whether true or not, it stands to reason that if God chose to share our human nature in Jesus Christ, then the flesh is something that we should rejoice in, along with everything else that God has created – as indeed our Lord plainly did. As a modern Anglican Franciscan Manual puts it:

The brothers and sisters . . . must remember that they follow the Son of Man, who came eating and drinking, who loved the birds and the flowers, who blessed little children, who was the friend of publicans and sinners, who sat at the tables alike of the rich and the poor. They will, therefore, put aside all gloom and moroseness, all undue aloofness from the common interests of people and delight in laughter and good fellowship. They will rejoice in God's world and all its beauty and its living creatures, calling nothing common or unclean.[6]

Another key idea for Catholics is that of '*belonging*'. I remember a friend of mine at university once saying to me shortly after he had become a Roman Catholic: 'All the things that we used to argue about as Anglicans, the Pope and the Blessed Virgin Mary and all the rest of it, somehow become secondary when you become a Catholic. What really matters is that you know that you are carried along in the great stream of the Church's life.' This sense of being 'carried along' is of course not confined to Roman Catholics. It is part of what it means to be an Orthodox Christian, and indeed Catholic Anglicans feel the same, though with an occasional sense of insecurity perhaps, through knowing that they are not fully accepted by the other two!

What is not so often realized is that behind this idea of 'belonging' there lies a whole 'scheme' of salvation. Every religion is of course about 'salvation' (and that includes modern secularism), in that every religion is about helping us out of our human predicament however that is conceived – lack of scientific know-how, ignorance, lack of enlightenment, enslavement to sin. The Christian Church has generally plumped for the last, but there have been markedly different ideas within the Church as to what is the best way out.

So, to take an obvious example, Evangelicals would say that the way out lies through the experience of 'conversion'. It is when we realize our true condition as sinners and in desperation turn to Christ, and then discover that in him we have a friend rather than a judge, who takes on himself the penalty of our sins and failures, that we are set free. This is the classic Evangelical experience – summed up in the phrase *'for me'*, the realization that it was 'for me' that he died. And Evangelical Church life is geared to this. Preaching, teaching, Bible study, individual witness, hymns and choruses all focus on getting people to realize their true state and then showing how in Jesus Christ God comes to our rescue. Basically it is a way of 'story telling' – of seeing the gospel as 'good news' to be shared – hence the great Evangelical concern with communication, whether by preaching or by the latest tool of audio visual technology. And the gospel *is*, of course, 'good news' – *the* good news. So, not surprisingly, it is a way which works well and one to which very many owe a great deal.

Catholic Christians also have their way out of the human predicament, and this as we have seen is the way of 'belonging'. It is different from the Evangelical way in that it often appears to be more low key and less challenging, and it is certainly more inclusive, with the Church seen as a 'school for sinners' rather than a 'society for saints'. But it can be truly said that everything is there for those who embark on this way. By 'belonging' we can discover eternal truths from the Church's teachings, be nourished by its sacraments, achieve holiness through its spiritual disciplines, find encouragement and support from fellow pilgrims, and be carried along by its life. The New Testament abounds with pictures which encourage us to see 'belonging' as the basic way forward – the Vine with its life-giving sap coursing through to the branches; the Body of Christ with its individual limbs and organs; the stones built to form a Temple in which the Spirit of God dwells. By 'belonging' you can find it all – including the 'good news' which is so crucial to the Evangelical way.

Of course the 'flip side' of this is that there is no guarantee that you will, and membership can all too easily remain an empty shell. This has always been the problem with the Catholic way – that it can degenerate into outward observance alone with no change within. There is a sense in which Catholics and Evangelicals need each other – Catholics to be reminded that conversion is part of the process of spiritual growth, and Evangelicals that human beings are complicated creatures and one kind of experience will not do for all. And perhaps both need other reminders – from Charismatics that the Spirit is a present and powerful reality, and from Liberals that nothing must be allowed to take the place of truth. This is not to say that 'Everyone has won, and all must have prizes!'[7] For in the last analysis only the Catholic way can contain all of these approaches. The others are in some sense reactions, usually because at some point Catholics have neglected a particular truth. In the end only the Catholic way is rich enough and varied enough to do justice to the full complexity and differing needs of human beings.

When it comes to what kind of body Catholics see themselves as belonging to, there is another keyword – '*universal*'. This is what 'catholic' actually means, and when we speak about 'the holy catholic Church' in the creed, we mean a

Church which is 'universal' in space and time. It is a Church which not only transcends geographical boundaries, but also stretches back in history to the first Apostles and even more significantly beyond the grave.

This is a mighty concept which gives a whole new dimension to that sense of belonging which all Catholics share. So the priest saying his daily office alone in his study is conscious of being part of a great stream of worship which flows continually to the very foot of God's throne – as are the one or two faithful at a weekday Eucharist, or the ordinary lay person at their prayers. And it is not confined to times of devotion. This is something which touches the whole of life. For it is something which can give immense confidence to people – even in situations of desperate isolation. To know that you are part of something so much bigger than yourself, something God given, something against which the 'gates of hell' can never prevail, is to know that special sense of belonging which Catholics so value.

But there is another side to this. Our hymn-books abound with triumphalist hymns about the Church, written many of them in the full flood of the Catholic revival, but we all know that the reality is very different. The institutional Church is going through a period of decline, especially in the West, and the Catholic part of it is no exception. Moreover many of the old certainties have gone too. Vatican II may have been a breath of fresh air for the Church, but it blew away many of the things that Catholics relied on for that feeling of confidence and security, which has always been one of the main attractions of Catholicism, particularly in its Roman form.

Many of us would see this as being a good thing – and a necessary thing if individuals are to have a mature faith. But that is not to say that what Bishop David Jenkins has called 'relaxed and relaxing belonging'[8] is not a good thing also. He sees the way forward as being 'in simple dependence upon God'. This is to go to the heart of the matter. For Catholics, as for any other Christian, the only real security is to be found in

God himself – in his faithfulness, and in his commitment to us and to his Church as his instrument in the world. All else is derivative. It is a hard lesson to learn, and it is not surprising that many Catholics (both Roman and Anglican) reject it in favour of defending old, secure positions. But if we can learn it, then we can relax in the certainty that however much the Church may change, however much it may be broken, purged, renewed, resurrected, its future and ours are in the hands of God, and that in the end is what matters.

Linked with this is another keyword, *'tradition'*. Catholic Christians have behind them a body of tradition which stretches back over twenty centuries. This is another aspect of 'belonging', of being carried along in the stream of the Church's life. At its best this enables the Church to stand outside its own generation, and to test and sift new ideas against a background of Christian wisdom down the ages. So it is able to reinterpret the gospel in the contemporary culture without being captured by it.

I say 'at its best' because in seeking to do this the Church always has to do battle on two fronts and has not always been successful in holding the line on either. On the one hand the influence of contemporary culture can be very pervasive. It has been said, for example, that even our 'ideas and images of God are themselves influenced and affected by the prevailing social order'.[9] Thus 'medieval ideas of God tend to stress order, while Reformation theology is concerned with the question of divine sovereignty', both reflecting the social and political concerns of the day. The same writer, Kenneth Leech, goes on to suggest that in today's world we hold a 'welfare conception of God', and that this fits in well with our ideas of social democracy. Certainly the way in which the clergy are grouped among the 'caring professions' in our contemporary culture lends force to this. And one might add that the way in which God is so often portrayed today as being only interested in morals and the private lives of individuals comes out of the same culture as Thatcherism, with its own particular emphasis on the individual and entrepreneurial values. There is of course no real harm in 'models' of this kind, provided that they are balanced by other models, if necessary from a different era, and that is where the strength of the Catholic tradition lies. It has a rich storehouse of models, and these can be pressed into service when a particular model shows signs of dominating the scene. We shall see the importance of this in connection with the healing ministry, particularly when we come to look at some of the wilder enthusiasms on offer in today's healing scene.

The opposite danger is for the Church to develop a siege mentality in the face of new ideas. The history of the Church is littered with examples of this – Galileo's persecution by the Inquisition for his views on astronomy is the classic instance. Even so it came as something of a shock to read of a Vatican announcement that the Roman Catholic Church had now given official recognition to the theory of evolution – in 1996! But all Churches have things to answer for here. The pressures to play safe, to preserve the status quo, are strong in any institution and particularly when that institution is under threat, as many Christians perceive the Church to be. It is not surprising that so many retreat into fundamentalism – whether of a Protestant or Catholic variety. This is doubly attractive as offering both a safe haven and a secure base from which to confront the uncertainties and agnosticism of our contemporary world. But it will not do. Fundamentalism, whether it be in an infallible Church or infallible Scriptures (or for that matter in the infallibility of rational thought), inevitably leads to a rigidity of mind which sooner or later fails to take account of the realities of life, and so fails those who look to the Church for help and salvation. As Bishop Rowan Williams has said: 'When we fail to speak to and to nourish the protesting, the doubting or the injured, God can be more catholic than we are.'[10]

In the end 'the tradition' must take its place with other contenders for our loyalty, when it comes to the decisions of day to day living. Nothing is infallible, and we have to find our way through life in humble dependence and trust in God's

Spirit, making use of the different things that he has given us to guide us. In fact many of the most exciting developments in the history of the Church seem to have found their inspiration from a wide variety of things – the Scriptures, the tradition of the Church, human knowledge, contemporary culture, the 'signs of the times', a personal call and the inspiration of God's Spirit. 'Look back, look out, and look up' is not a bad recipe for living, and certainly there have been times when it has changed the course of history.

Perhaps the last word on tradition and its connection with Catholicism comes from the former Archbishop of York, Dr John Habgood. Writing after the unfortunate Bennett affair of 1987, he said:

In the long-term the future lies with Catholicism. It must, because only Catholic tradition is rich enough and stable enough to be able to offer something distinctive to the world without being captured by the world. But it must be a Catholicism which is true to its highest vision, and hence broad enough, hospitable enough, rooted sufficiently in sacramental reality, confident enough in its inheritance to be able to do new things, diverse enough, and yet passionately enough concerned about unity, to be genuinely universal.[11]

Undoubtedly for most ordinary people the really distinctive thing about Catholicism (whether Anglican or Roman Catholic) is its style of *worship*. It is true that differences have become blurred since Vatican II, with the dropping of Latin and the growth of the Parish Mass/Family Eucharist movement across the denominational boundaries. Gone are the days of the non-communicating High Mass as the Anglo-Catholic alternative to 'Establishment Matins'! Nevertheless Catholic worship does remain distinctive, even with these developments. And this distinctiveness is characterized by another keyword – *'Presence'*. I remember towards the end of the last war receiving a Christmas card from the father of a school friend of mine, who was an Anglo-Catholic vicar, and in whose dilapidated vicarage I had stayed during the summer holidays. It depicted a priest and servers at mass, half hidden in a cloud of incense, and above them hovering within the cloud were Mary and Joseph with the child Jesus and the angels and shepherds. Underneath were the words of a well-known hymn:

> I see thee not, I hear thee not,
> Yet art thou oft with me;
> And earth hath ne'er so dear a spot
> As where I meet with thee.[12]

This seemed then, and still seems to me, to sum up what is special about Catholic worship – that it is centred on the mysterious Presence of the Lord, whether that presence is to be found at the Eucharist, or signified by the light burning before the tabernacle or aumbry. One thinks automatically of some dimly lit Victorian church, where a waft of incense remains on the air, and the lamp flickers in the gloom above the high altar or in the quiet of a side chapel. However while atmosphere certainly heightens the sense of mystery, the reality of the Presence is not dependent on this. As David Stancliffe, the present Bishop of Salisbury, once put it rather bluntly at an Affirming Catholicism Conference: 'Catholics believe that something happens in church, Protestants do not'![13]

It is perhaps worth spending a little time thinking about church architecture and furnishings, because they do provide clues as to what the worshippers think are important. Take a medieval church, for example: almost half of it is often given over to chancel and sanctuary. Here is an empty space waiting to be filled, waiting for the Presence at the time of the Eucharist. How different from the purpose-built Protestant chapel, with its central pulpit and lectern, its rows of seats and its gallery. The one is a shrine, the other an auditorium. Both express very different ideas about the purpose of being there. And one could go on. I have taken confirmations in a Charismatic church which was so full of electronic gear that one could hardly move. But it expressed very clearly how the congregation saw the purpose of worship – continuous praise, praise expressed through exuberant and triumphalist song, praise assisted and enlarged by every device of modern technology that one could think of. Even an Orthodox church has its own particular nuance when it comes to architecture and furnishings. Here the sense is not so much that of being in a shrine, as of being taken out of this world. The iconostasis with its well-known saints, the pictures and relics of local holy men and women, the giant figure of Christ the Pantocrator under the dome, all contribute to this. Indeed the Orthodox call their icons 'windows of heaven', and see their liturgy as a time when the faithful are lifted up to share in the worship of heaven. Here is a quite different concept from the Catholic one, though a complementary one, reflecting the Orthodox's theological focus on the resurrection which we have already noted.

Thoughts about worship lead naturally to thoughts about the sacraments, and *'sacramental'* is another Catholic keyword. In fact it has been said that if you ask a Catholic what is the 'bottom line' of his or her spirituality, he or she will often answer that it is the objectivity of the sacraments which really matters – that when you receive holy communion or absolution or whatever, the gift of grace that goes with it is *guaranteed*. That is fine, particularly for those 'off' mornings when you have a headache or are not feeling very religious, *provided always* that it is remembered that the phrase 'gift of grace' is actually another way of describing the *generosity* of the Holy One at the heart of creation. I have heard sermons on the sacraments based on signing blank cheques or turning on a tap, and that simply will not do. That is how the sacraments so easily become confused with magic, and the Reformers were right to protest against such ideas. But equally the sacraments cannot be downgraded, as some Protestant teaching would have them, as 'merely subjective'. They are God's love gifts to us, and as such certainly have a guaranteed quality about them. But of course to move them from the mechanical plane into that of the personal actually bypasses the old Catholic/Protestant argument about objective and subjective. To be at the receiving end of another's generosity is to become part of a circle of loving giving and loving response in which the objective and subjective cannot really be distinguished. Every sacrament is a person to person thing, and we forget that at our peril.

All this has bearing on the ministry of healing, but there is much more to the Catholic idea of 'sacramental' than 'the sacraments'. 'Sacramental' describes a whole way of looking at life. 'The whole of creation is our guru, our teacher', writes Donald Nicholl,[14] and Philip Sheldrake in a memorable phrase speaks of our being 'God's body language'.

Somebody (and I cannot remember who) described our own bodies and our bodily desires as God's own body language, and that is a very strongly sacramental understanding of embodiment. We need to listen to the language of our own bodies. The body, my body, your body, our bodies, are sacraments of our own identity; but also our bodies are sacraments of God's presence and reality to me.[15]

Here is an invitation to see below the surface of things to the mystery that lies beneath even the most ordinary of objects. And it has very practical consequences. It means that neither individual human beings nor God himself are limited to the verbal – to words. In fact the deepest communication often occurs through the simplest of gestures – a touch of the hand, a smile, or (negatively) an avoiding of the eyes. And when the time came for God to reveal himself, he chose to do it through a human life. We shall see the importance of this for the ministry of healing in due course, but it is one of the particular contributions that Catholics have to make to this ministry, over against the Protestant dependence on words and verbal communication.

Catholics also have a contribution to make through their rich tradition of *spirituality*. Here is to be found the accumulated experience and wisdom of saints and mystics, spiritual directors, solitaries, Church leaders, humble parish priests, and ordinary men and women. And it is a tradition which continues to grow and flourish. Books on prayer and the spiritual life sell well, whether they are classics from former centuries or modern compilations. And their influence extends well beyond normal Church circles. Sister Wendy Beckett, Gerard Hughes, Mother Teresa are all to be found in secular bookshops, and not necessarily on the shelves marked 'Religion'. It is one of the signs of the times that people are hungry for spiritual knowledge, and especially any spiritual knowledge that can contribute to their development as a person, or help them through the difficulties and pains that are the normal lot of most of us at some time or another.

Of course books on prayer and spirituality are not the preserve of Catholics. Other traditions have their spiritual writers too, and one of the signs of a real growing together among the Churches is the way in which people have begun to value and respect the spiritual riches of others. But sometimes theology can get in the way. Evangelicals, for example, usually have far less to say about 'growth' in the spiritual life than Catholics or Orthodox. The emphasis on conversion as *the* event in a person's life has a way of downgrading all subsequent events. In addition Evangelicals are rightly suspicious of anything that smacks of earning your way into God's favour by good works. So Bishop Ryle, an early Evangelical Bishop of Liverpool, writes:

Genuine Scriptural holiness will make a man do his duty at home and by the fireside . . . It will make a man humble, kind, gentle, unselfish, good-tempered, considerate for others, loving, meek, and forgiving . . . It will not constrain him to go out of the world, and shut himself up in a cave like a hermit.[16]

Here is a worthy but limited vision. It is one which takes little account of the uniqueness of individual vocations, and even less of God's occasional use of heroic gestures to change his world.

A different but possibly more damaging limitation is to be found amongst Charismatics. It is a well-known fact that Charismatics, with their emphasis on the triumphant power of the Spirit, find failure and defeat very difficult to cope with. The agonizing which went on over David Watson's death is a case in point. I can remember being at a Lent meeting once at which a group from an Oxford church described how they praised God for everything that came their way, and at which a woman spoke of the death of her mother in a manner which seemed to ignore all the normal feelings of bereavement. Next day I had a distressed phone call from a doctor friend, who had been there. He was as Charismatic as any of them – in fact he later joined a local Charismatic community with his family – but he also suffered from bouts of severe depression, which nothing seemed able to shift. 'They never grow up', was his comment, and I shall never forget the bitterness with which he said it. He felt that he had been let down by people who should have understood – his problem pushed aside, minimalized, because it didn't fit in with their particular recipe for living.

So once again we need each other, and it is heartening to see the way that Christians of all traditions are now discovering the spiritual riches outside their own. David Gillett, who has published a definitive account of Evangelical spirituality in his book *Trust and Obey*, writes:

Given an attitude to one's own spiritual tradition which is thankful but critical, iconoclastic yet affirming, we can begin to benefit from the greater openness to other traditions which is such a feature of the pluralism of our age. It is something to be welcomed as a gift and opportunity from God, rather than to be feared and rejected as an unwelcome feature of our culture.[17]

I find it immensely exciting, for example, suddenly to discover a book by an Evangelical on silence, or by a Charismatic on spiritual discipline, or to read in a *Renewal* magazine an article on St John of the Cross. This last contained advice for

Charismatics on what to do when your prayers go 'dead' on you! Equally I find a richness and warmth in many of Charles Wesley's hymns which speak to my condition in a way which much Catholic spirituality does not. And with more modern hymn writers too. It was Graham Kendrick's hymn 'The Servant King', sung just before the sermon at what I think was the most triumphalist Institution Service I have ever taken part in, which caused me to depart radically from my prepared text a few minutes later!

> Come, see his hands
> And his feet,
> The scars that speak
> Of sacrifice,
> Hands that flung stars
> Into space
> To cruel nails
> Surrendered.[18]

Here is a Charismatic spirituality which does make space for what some have called the 'mystery' of success and failure, which my doctor friend so wanted to hear, and which I guess some in that congregation wanted to hear too.

There are two further bits of the Catholic mosaic which need to be considered before it can in any way be said to be complete. The first is the Catholic tradition of *social work*. This has always been there – St Francis, for example, stands in a long line of individuals which stretches right up to the present day with such people as Mother Teresa and Jean Vanier of the l'Arche Communities. For Anglican Catholics it is the slum priests around the turn of the century, who are the particular embodiments of this – Frs Lowder, Wainwright, Stanton, Wilson, Mackonochie, Williamson and many others. Their biographies still make compelling reading and the extent of their dedication (Fr Wainwright for example never spent a single night outside his parish during his long ministry there) is quite astonishing. It is doubtful if they theologized much about their work – they just got on with the job in the belief that God had called them to be priests and pastors in places where no one else would go, and more specifically where normal Church of England methods didn't work. But Christian social work is in fact a direct consequence of that Catholic emphasis on the incarnation which we have already noted. It was Henry Scott Holland who said: 'The more you believe in the Incarnation, the more you care about drains'.[19] And parallel with the work of the slum priests was the work of several groups of Anglican Catholics who certainly did theologize about social matters – Henry Scott Holland, Charles Gore, B. F. Westcott amongst others. 'Christ came to redeem the whole world of matter and nothing less than the redemption of the whole world should be the concern of Catholics.' We shall see how this broadens any concept of a ministry of healing when we come to consider 'Our Sick Society' in Chapter 8.

Catholics also have a tradition of *evangelism*, and no picture of Catholic belief and practice is complete without this. For those of us who are Anglicans, and whose ministry began in the 1950s, this has always been typified by the brothers and sisters of the Society of St Francis. I remember during one of the missions to Oxford University, when Fr Algy and Br Peter were billeted on Exeter College, an Evangelical ordinand, who is now a noted evangelist, saying with surprise (and approval), 'But these men really preach the gospel'! In fact Catholic evangelism is usually somewhat more low key – hence the confusing word 'evangelisation' which the Roman Catholics have coined for it. It has always depended rather more on getting people to commit themselves to regular worship and other forms of spiritual discipline than on sudden conversions. But this commitment can be a powerful agent for inner conversion. Most Anglo-Catholic missions of the traditional kind majored on confession, and to make a first confession could very often be as much a sign of inner change as any response to an evangelist's call to 'come forward'. Certainly it required as much

courage, if not more! More importantly, Catholic faith and practice has built into it a powerful witness over against the world
and against conventional religion – weekly attendance at the
Eucharist, confession, spiritual direction, retreats, fasting, a
high doctrine of priesthood, monks and nuns, not to mention
its ritual externals (now thankfully toned down in most
places!). It was this sense that Catholics 'meant business' by
their religion, as opposed to ordinary 'C of E' members, that
drew many of us to this tradition at a formative time in our
lives.

So here is the Catholic 'mosaic'. Talk of 'mosaics' with
their 'shapes' and 'patterns' means that this chapter, as expected, has been mainly impressionistic, rather than a systematic
treatment of Catholic faith and practice. I suspect, however,
that we shall probably get further by starting in this way than
if we had taken another road. Theology is important, but its
importance in any given instance is often revealed as much
through impressions and the 'feel' of things, as through rational thought. And, as has already been hinted, the whole area of
healing is notoriously untidy when it comes to theological systems. My own feeling is that insights and impressions are likely
to serve us better, as we come to explore 'healing' in all its many
aspects in the rest of this book.

2 A Modern Miracle

Christian attitudes to medicine

Medicine is perhaps the last and purest bastion of
Enlightenment dreams, tying together, reason, science, and
the dream of unlimited human possibilities. There is nothing, it is held, that in principle cannot be done and, given
suitable caution, little that ought not to be done.

(Daniel Callahan, 'Setting Limits: Medical Goals in an
Aging Society')[1]

D URING THE SCARLET FEVER epidemic of 1856 the Dean of
Carlisle, Archibald Tait, wrote in the front of his Prayer
Book: 'I used this book at the funerals of my dearest children
Charlotte and Susan on 10th and 12th March 1856'. A little later
he wrote below it: 'Also – alas! of my sweet Frances on Good
Friday the 21st and of my eldest born, my darling sainted Catty
on Wednesday after Easter the 26th, the day after the anniversary of her baptism.' And again later: 'Also – woe's me – how
shall I write it – of my bright Mary on the 10th of April.' Within
the space of a few weeks the disease had carried off all five of
his daughters, leaving him and his wife with one son, who later
died at the age of twenty-nine.

It would be hard to find a more dramatic illustration of
the way things have changed since Victorian times. Dean Tait's
losses were counted a tragedy even then, but childhood deaths
were common. One prominent Victorian is said to have
declared that he always avoided becoming too emotionally
involved with his children because he knew that he would lose
one of them sooner or later. Even in this century right up to the
postwar period, this was still not an unusual occurrence

amongst poorer families. I can remember as late as the 1960s, in my estate parish in Sunderland which housed families from the town's old east end, asking people how many children they had and frequently getting a reply such as: 'Four – and I buried two'. And a friend of mine who was a GP in Hull told me how working-class mothers choosing clothes for their children in the chain stores would always go for those that could 'dye black'. How different things are today. The childhood killer diseases are a thing of the past. Measles, whooping cough, diphtheria, polio have all yielded to massive immunization programmes, and when you hear of a child dying nowadays it is nearly always from something else – cancer, muscular dystrophy, or some rare and unusual disease. Or there has been a mistake. And always it is seen as something exceptional, and something we have lost the means of coping with.

What is true of expectations in childhood is also true of adult life. I was unfortunate enough to contract TB in 1949 during my national service and spent nine months in hospital. The treatment then was largely rest, either actual rest or artificially induced through collapsing the affected lung. And the prevailing expectation amongst those of us who were patients was that sooner or later we would be back again, perhaps to have something more drastic and unpleasant done to us (the thoracoplasty was the great dread, with harrowing accounts by those who had had it of rib breaking under local anaesthetic). In fact of course the discovery of streptomycin and other drugs changed everything. Within a few years I found that the sanatorium where I used to go for X-ray and check-up was full of heart patients. And when I did come across TB again in a hospital where I was chaplain in Sunderland, the average stay was about eight weeks.

One could go on illustrating what, in the words of the title for this chapter, really is a 'modern miracle', with disease after disease. Polio, for example, the other great dread of young men and women in the first half of this century, has yielded to the Salk vaccine. And antibiotics have altered our ways of coping with many other diseases which were killers in the past. One statistic has it that whereas in 1930 eighty per cent of deaths in this country were from infectious diseases and only twenty per cent from chronic ones, by 1970 the position had exactly reversed – twenty per cent from infectious diseases and eighty per cent from chronic ones. And all this has been matched by advances in surgery and medical technology, which would have been regarded as pure science fiction a hundred years ago – kidney, liver and heart transplants, brain surgery, hip and knee replacements, heart and lung machines, full body scanners, micro-surgery, and many other techniques. It is a sobering thought that at the turn of the century, when Edward VII developed appendicitis, the removal of his appendix under anaesthetic was regarded as a highly dangerous and unusual procedure. We have come a long way since then.

Yet it has not all been an unmitigated success story. In the first place it is mainly people in the developed world who have benefited from all these advances. Big strides have been made in the rest of the world, notably in the eradication of smallpox, but it remains true that in poorer countries the majority of people have only a limited access to Western medicine despite the efforts of the World Health Organisation. And even in developing countries it can be very much a hit and miss affair. I once heard a doctor describe the few months that he had spent in one of the prestige hospitals built in Colonel Gaddafi's Libya. It was stuffed full of all the latest technological equipment, but when you turned on a tap no water came out, or if it did it was contaminated! The West remains in a very privileged position as far as health care is concerned.

Then it must be remembered that many of the really big strides that have been made have been in the realm of prevention rather than cure. Clean water, better housing and improved sanitation early in the century were major contributors to the virtual extinction in this country of such diseases as cholera and to the reduction of childhood mortality in general. Immunization programmes also played their part, as did early diagnosis. It is not often realized that the death rate from TB plummeted between 1900 and 1950 due to mass X-ray and also to better housing and nutrition, and that the advent of strepto- mycin at the end of the Second World War made little difference to the figures for those actually dying from the disease. What it did do of course was to reduce the treatment time and so free resources for other needs. There is a certain glamour attached to 'wonder drugs' and advanced surgical techniques, which has a perennial appeal, and which is continually fed by the media. While achievements in the realm of curative medicine should not be underestimated, it yet remains true that the actual story is a good deal less glamorous, and in one sense all of a doctor's work still consists in helping nature work its own cure.

As it happens the medical world is going through something of a difficult period at the moment. Part of the trouble is that doctors have become the victims of their own success. Having eradicated most of the old killer diseases, they are left with those like cancer and multiple sclerosis, which do not yield so readily to treatment. Or with unglamourous tasks such as coping with the growing number of elderly people. Or with notable failures such as not finding a cure for AIDS. Or with the results of their own mistakes such as new strains of old diseases which are resistant to normal treatments because of the misuse of antibiotics and other drugs. These are the things which tend to come under the spotlight now rather than the successes of the past. And then there is the matter of unfulfilled expectations. When Beveridge produced his famous report in 1942 it was confidently predicted that the reduction in disease would keep spending on health within manageable limits. Both he and Aneurin Bevan, the Minister of Health at the time of the inauguration of the Health Service in 1948, assumed that the service would be 'self-eliminating' and that as the years passed and the nation's health improved the demand for health care would become less. This of course has not happened. In fact in every country in the Western world the reverse has occurred. As we have seen chronic diseases which do not yield to simple treatments have taken the place of the old killer diseases. Expectations of a better quality of life and an ageing population have led to increased demands for health care. And advances in technology have caused the cost of treatments to escalate. As a result resources have become strained, and certainly in this country with a National Health Service now visibly struggling to provide universal care from cradle to grave, people are beginning to feel that things are no longer what they were. Add to this the general trend in society towards the 'debunking' of authority figures, and the increasing emphasis on an individual's 'rights', and it can be easily understood why the medical profession does not feel as secure as it once did. I heard recently, for example, that the average obstetrician now has something like forty lawsuits on his or her books at any one time. Most of these do not come to court, but it is an indication of the way attitudes are changing.

Not all the changes are negative however. One more positive change is the shift by many doctors away from treating the body as a machine and medicine as a technique to a more 'holistic' approach. That is certainly to be welcomed. It remains an uphill struggle however, and there are several reasons for this. In the first place, the training doctors receive is in the opposite direction. The 'reductionist' approach, which focuses on gaining maximum knowledge through specialization, has been brilliantly successful as a way of advancing medical science, and this still dominates medical education. Indeed the specialists in medical schools, brilliant as they may be in their own subject, are often ill-equipped to teach the care of the whole person, even if they wanted to. Then there is the framework within which doctors are expected to work. 'Person centred' medicine has always been very much part of General Practice, and in theory this is now being specifically encouraged by the Health Service. I say 'in theory', because in practice the latter seems to be sending out confusing signals. On the one hand publications like *Making Time for Patients* clearly favour a 'whole person' model rather than a 'cure' model of health care, but on the other the actual burdens placed on doctors and nurses in terms of workload and time that can be given to patients make this very difficult to fulfil in practice. I know of one GP who back in the seventies always watched to see if patients hesitated when they put their hand on the door knob. If they did he would ask: 'Are you sure you have told me what you really came about?' The result sometimes played havoc with his surgery timetable, but he felt that it was worth it. Today many GPs would say that they simply haven't got the time for this kind of thing, much as they would like to be able to do it. Finally there is the matter of professional competence. Many doctors feel uncomfortable at the whole idea of 'holistic' medicine, knowing that they would be out of their depth as soon as 'illnesses' started to turn into 'problems'. This was something that they had received no training for, and should not therefore be expected to deal with. Yet, with all these difficulties, at the end of the day the 'whole person' approach must be the way forward to true health, if only because we are more than the sum of our parts and everything about us is affected by everything else. As one doctor has written of his own methods in the consulting room:

The spoken word is the royal road to human understanding in medicine. It is the difference between 'knowing that' or 'knowing how' and 'knowing whom' or 'knowing whether'. It is the difference between medicine as sophisticated veterinarianism and a distinctly human science and art.[2]

I have dwelt on all this at length because I do believe very strongly that any book on a Christian approach to healing must start with this 'miracle' of modern medicine. And in spite of all the difficulties and uncertainties which afflict the medical world today, 'miracle' is the right word. The plain fact is that many of us reading these pages would be dead were it not for secular medicine – born dead, possibly, or succumbing to something quite simply dealt with today like an inflamed appendix!

And what would life be like without pain-killers? None of us can afford to adopt a superior or grudging attitude towards the achievements of medical science – though sadly some Christians have been known to. Deep thankfulness coupled with sheer wonder are more like what we should be feeling if we have any imagination at all, and any thoughts on a Christian approach to healing must start with this.

One general result of this 'modern miracle' has been to alter totally the way most human beings now regard sickness. It is not often realized how recent a phenomenon this is or how differently our forebears coped with serious illness. Yet it was only in the eighteenth century that the scientific method really began to be applied to medicine, and antiseptic surgery and vaccination had to wait another hundred years. Indeed even up to the middle of the last century doctors were still using the old treatments of purgation, bleeding and cupping in the false belief that these stimulated the body to fight disease. No wonder that the prevailing attitude in the face of serious illness was usually one of fatalistic acceptance. The Prayer Book reflects this attitude very plainly in its Visitation of the Sick:

Whatsoever your sickness is, know you certainly, that it is God's visitation ... And ... that if you truly repent you of your sins, and bear your sickness patiently, ... it shall turn to your profit ... For whom the Lord loveth he chasteneth.

This all changed dramatically with the advent of modern medicine. Once you could do something about being ill, things felt very different. Safe surgery, treatments which really worked because they were based on the scientific study of how the body functioned, and eventually in the second half of this century drugs which actually destroyed invading organisms, very quickly altered the whole way people regarded sickness. They began to expect doctors to cure them. Fatalistic acceptance was replaced by high expectations, until now we have a situation in which the doctor's ability to make us better is virtually taken for granted, and we feel that there is something very wrong if this does not prove to be the case.

It is interesting to see how the Churches adjusted to this change of attitude. In one way of course many Christians felt that the Churches didn't need to adjust at all. The physical and the spiritual had been separated for so long that in many people's minds the business of healing people could be safely left to doctors and hospitals and the Church's role limited to prayer and spiritual support. Yet that would not really do. What were you to pray for – acceptance that this sickness was God's will for you, or that you might get better? After all that was why you had gone to the doctor – to get better! It was not surprising that thinking people soon started to question the traditional teaching of the Church that sickness was something to be accepted passively. And then there was the matter of new knowledge. When you knew scientifically that your illness was caused by nasty little germs rather than by some sort of divine visitation, it all began to look rather different. Perhaps God was against germs too, and could be enlisted in the fight against them. And then came the discovery (or rather rediscovery) that Jesus also seemed to be against sickness, and that a good deal of his ministry was taken up with battling against it. People began to notice how the Gospels showed the conquest of disease as one of the signs of the Kingdom, and how the Lord himself unmistakably charged his Church not only to preach but to heal the sick.

As so often happens this change within the Church began in a small way and with individuals. But by the turn of the century a number of prophetic voices were beginning to be heard and traditional views challenged. It was as early as 1904 that Dr Percy Dearmer, known to generations of clergymen as the author of *The Parson's Handbook*, with Conrad Noel and others, started the Guild of Health. The Society of Emmanuel (later The Divine Healing Mission) followed in 1905, and the Guild of St Raphael in 1915. All these in their different ways reflected a new and more militant approach to sickness and were dedicated to the revival of the healing ministry as an integral part of the Church's life. Meanwhile 'centres' of healing were also springing up, again usually around particular individuals. In 1912 a girl of twenty-three, who had been an invalid for five years, was miraculously healed when she was near death. Indeed the medical evidence of the time states that her breathing ceased and her heart stopped beating for eight minutes and that her consumptive lungs appeared to have been replaced with new ones. Dorothy Kerin herself certainly believed that her healing came from God and that she had been entrusted with a message to the world, 'a promise of healing to the sick, comfort to the sorrowing and faith to the faithless.'[3] Her inspiration led to the founding of the Community and Church of Christ the Healer at Burrswood, dedicated to the Church and the medical profession working in close harmony – the first of an increasing number of healing centres.

It took the Church a little time to respond in its official bodies to this movement. As far as the Anglican Church was concerned the matter was discussed as early as 1908 by the Lambeth Conference, and again in 1920, when a committee was set up 'to consider and report upon the use with prayer of the laying on of hands, of the Unction of the sick, and other spiritual means of healing'.[4] The committee reported in 1924 and the 1930 Lambeth Conference commended the whole report, though it was hesitant on the subject of 'public Missions of Healing'. As one commentator has since stated: 'For the first time that I know of, a modern mainline church acknowledged in an official pronouncement that unction and laying on of hands can have a direct effect on the body.'[5]

From then on there was increasing recognition not only within the Anglican Church, but in the other Churches as well, of the importance of this ministry and of this changed attitude to sickness. Perhaps one of the most significant changes occurred within the Roman Catholic Church, which as a result of the Second Vatican Council (1962-5) restored the sacrament of extreme unction to its original purpose as a healing sacrament and renamed it 'The Anointing of the Sick'. Today most of the mainline Churches encourage some kind of ministry of healing as part of their official policy and the movement continues to grow.

How should Christians and the Churches regard secular medicine? That is a key question which strangely enough does not get a lot of attention in the majority of books on Christian healing. Granted that our starting point ought to be the one already mentioned of deep thankfulness and wonder at the achievements of medical science, nevertheless secular medicine is *secular*, and therefore the relationship between the two can never be completely straightforward. Medical science and Christianity do share many values, but there are also subtle differences, and many of these are becoming more and more apparent as society in general sheds its Christian heritage and becomes more secular.

The first thing to be said in answer to this question is that there is no one 'Christian' way of relating to secular medicine. Christians vary very considerably as to how they regard it, from almost total acceptance at one end of the scale to virtually ignoring it at the other. Generally speaking however there are two common approaches. On the one hand there is the approach which treats medicine as a separate compartment of life from 'religion' – important, vital even, but having nothing directly to do with the real business of religion, which is 'salvation'. I once asked an Evangelical consultant how he regarded secular medicine, and after a lot of thought he came up with the phrase: 'Well, neutral, I suppose'. The other approach makes no such distinction and endeavours to include medicine within its definition of 'religion'. 'I give injections as a prayer' – so said a district nurse. Notice that what she said was, '*as a* prayer', not '*with* prayer' (though no doubt she did pray as well on many such occasions). The thought is of the actual physical business of sticking a needle into someone for their benefit being itself a prayer, an act of worship, an act of co-operation with the Creator in the healing of his creation.

Generally speaking Liberals and Catholics are more at home with this latter approach; Evangelicals and Charismatics with the former. This is by no means a hard and fast rule. There is for example a wealth of Catholic literature which speaks of people as *'souls'*, as there is also a Catholic tradition of spirituality which sees this life as important only as a preparation for eternity. But leaving that aside, it is true to say that theologically Catholics and Liberals are generally more predisposed to a *world-affirming* view of medicine than Evangelicals and Charismatics. This comes out very clearly in the 'bridge' organizations which are representative of the two groups. The Evangelical Doctors' and Nurses' Christian Fellowships, for example, tend to focus on the conversion of individuals, and operate in very similar ways to the Evangelical student 'Fellowships' in universities. By contrast the Institute of Religion and Medicine and its successor the Medical Forum of the Churches' Council for Health and Healing have always been much more concerned with *issues* – doctor/clergy cooperation, values within medicine, and actual Health Service decisions. These differences are basically theological, and it is this that we must consider, if we are to understand why these different approaches take the form that they do.

What are these theological differences? In essence they stem from something that we have already drawn attention to – that Evangelical theology is *cross* centred, while Catholic theology is *incarnation* centred. To take Catholic theology first, as we saw in the first chapter, the fact that the Word was made *flesh* has inevitable consequences as to how we view God's creation. The natural world and the world of everyday life has a validity in its own right. It is not just spiritual things that count. So what happens to our bodies, to society, to nature itself insofar as it is used or abused is important to God the Creator, and part of a balanced spirituality is recognizing this and the responsibilities that go with it. Donald Nicholl has a delightful story in his book on *Holiness*, in which he tells of a woman he saw in church who struck a wasp dead with a rolled-up newspaper, just as the priest was saying in the mass: 'Blessed art Thou, Lord, God of all creation'![6] This prayer, and the act of offering which accompanies it, implies that everyday things have a *theological* and *spiritual* dimension, and this includes major things like secular medicine as well as how we treat wasps! Medicine too is something that we bless God for as part of his creation – or possibly seek to change, in those areas where it seems to be moving in directions contrary to his will.

A further aspect of this is that Catholics find it natural to see God at work in all that is good in his creation. Christ is 'the true light which gives light to everyone', and his Spirit is by no means confined to the Church and to believers. So God is seen to be behind the achievements of medical science as well as the self-giving and dedication of many doctors and nurses – whether they recognize the fact or not. This inevitably paves the way for a more co-operative and accepting approach to secular medicine, as indeed it does to some forms of complementary medicine, particularly when these are linked to an ancient Faith. It is no accident, for example, that Catholic contemplatives, like Thomas Merton and Bede Griffiths, find themselves being drawn to mystics of other Faiths. At the deep level of prayer they discover that they have a natural affinity with them, and in consequence recognize the 'true light' within, even though the dogmas underlying their respective religions are quite different. So such therapies as yoga, acupuncture, and Eastern meditation are not automatically condemned by Catholics, though they may well have cautions about certain aspects of them. As Dr John Habgood has said: 'Catholicism tells us of a big God who is present in unexpected places'.[7]

Evangelicals by contrast have rarely been 'world-affirming' having, in the words of one of their writers on spirituality, 'not given pride of place to the doctrines of creation and incarnation'.

Indeed, evangelicals have tended to emphasize ... the concept of original sin, thus giving more prominence to the fall tradition than to the original blessing of God's good creation. The fall, rather than creation, has a clear place within the evangelical tradition because it is the essential foundation in any evangelical doctrine of the cross.[8]

In many ways the fallenness of our human nature – that built-in twist which so often seems to turn even our best endeavours to dust and ashes – is something that we need to be reminded of. Indeed Catholics have often been criticized for having too optimistic a view of human nature. This is certainly true of that strain of teaching which held that our reason was unaffected by the fall. The Reformers were right to insist that this was also corrupted, and modern psychology, with its insights into how easily we rationalize things so that they fit our way of thinking, bears this out. Not that one needs psychologists to point this out. One of my more frightening insights came from a snippet on the car radio at the end of a chat show. A journalist, who had just been reminded that he belonged to a profession which 'moulded public opinion', came back with the devastating reply: 'We don't mould public opinion, we confirm prejudices!' More recently the spotlight has been turned on the biologists with their talk of the 'selfish' gene.[9] This is a phrase which is easily misunderstood, as it is really just a graphic way of describing how we are programmed genetically within the process of natural selection. But the phrase is a suggestive one, and is yet another reminder that none of us enter this world with a totally clean sheet. Life will always be a struggle to rise above both what we have inherited as part of our make-up, and the influences from outside that have moulded us during our formative years. So we should not be surprised that the story of medicine, for all its splendid record of human dedication and self-giving, shows evidence of this built-in twist in human nature just as everything else does. And we owe it to Evangelicals for reminding us of this. It is not a particularly fashionable or popular way of looking at things in our modern secular world with its naive belief in human progress, but then popularity has never had a very high priority with

Evangelicals! In David Gillett's phrase, Evangelical teaching 'will always manifest a certain grain-in-the-oyster-shell quality'.[10] But without such grains there would be no pearls.

However other aspects of this theological emphasis are less helpful. The trouble is that if you focus on sin and the need for conversion, it can very quickly lead to a downgrading of everything else as secondary. If your main mission in life is, in the words of one of Sankey's hymns, to:

> Go forth, and rescue those that perish,
> Where sin and darkness reign ...[11]

then only one thing really matters – to 'pluck brands from the burning'. Of course this is something of a caricature, but as John Goldingay, the former Principal of the Evangelical college of St John's, Nottingham has said: 'Evangelicalism is instinctively pietistic'.[12] Evangelicals have never been wholly at ease with what is *natural*, and this world and its concerns have never mattered to them in quite the same way that they have to Catholics or Liberals.

When one comes to compare the differences between Catholics and Liberals in their approach to secular medicine the picture is less clear. It is however in the area of God's activity, and in particular his activity through the sacraments, that the clearest 'stretch of blue water' between them is to be found. For example one hospital chaplain, who would have styled himself a 'Liberal', once said to me of anointing: 'I do it to make them feel good!' That is a very different expectation from the Catholic one of the risen Christ present in his power to heal. Liberals, by contrast to Catholics, are nearly always suspicious of any kind of 'supernatural' activity. They look to a God who works only through 'normal channels'. The good side of this is that it makes them take their duty as critics of the status quo very seriously. And this is reinforced by their focus on our Lord's ministry, which we have already noted. Jesus is seen as prophet, teacher and example, and the Gospel events are taken seriously as theological and prophetic comment on today's situation. So secular medicine and all that goes with it comes under the scrutiny and judgement of the gospel. Liberals never make the mistake of some Catholics of ignoring the importance of normal everyday living and the decisions that go with it. Their hope is always to influence these and thereby change things, and so (in one of their favourite phrases) to bring in the *Kingdom* – those conditions, that set of circumstances, that place, where God's values, God's will, God's rule hold sway.

Interestingly it is often in the matter of externals that the Catholic concern with the supernatural and the spiritual becomes most apparent. Nurses, for example, know to call the Roman Catholic priest when one of his flock is dying. And they know that the call out is for the 'last rites'. So the whole concept of eternity is introduced into the secular atmosphere of the hospital ward. Anglican Catholic chaplains have struggled down the years to get a similar recognition from ward staff, but have largely failed. In the fifties and sixties when I did some chaplaincy work, the prevailing culture in the hospitals that I had dealings with seemed only to stretch to call outs for emergency baptisms. It took a very firm request from a patient or relatives for the Anglican chaplain to be called out for anything else. And the present emphasis on patients' rights will not have made things any easier. However this is not all loss, as emergency baptism has its own witness, as does the giving of holy communion on the wards. And there is a similar witness from such simple things as praying with people and blessing them at the end of a visit. All of these in their different ways show that spiritual things actually matter to people, that they have a part in their total wellbeing. More than that, for those who have any knowledge of the beliefs that lie behind them, they are also a direct challenge in a very practical way to many of the assumptions which undergird secular medicine.

However the area where Catholic beliefs and practice probably mount the strongest challenge to secular medicine is in the realm of medical ethics. Everyone knows, for example,

that the Roman Catholic Church has strong views on contra-
ception and abortion, and that doctors and nurses are able to
exercise a right of conscience not to participate in abortions
under the 1967 Act. Other matters which they also feel strongly about include euthanasia, for which there is growing support
in our society, and the whole 'Pandora's Box' of human fertilization and embryology. A string of papal encyclicals and
other directives have made it very plain where the Roman
Catholic Church stands on these issues, and this has had a
direct effect on medical practice in countries such as Ireland,
where the Church's influence is still strong. Roman Catholics of
course are not the only Christians who take a strong line.
Evangelicals have their 'pro-life' supporters, and most
Christians are concerned about these issues and some of the
practices allowed in connection with them, even when they feel
that they cannot go the whole way with the 'pro-life' lobby.

How are we to view the Roman Catholic stance? To
take abortion as an example, many Anglican Catholics, like
Anglicans in general, would want to take a less stringent line
and be prepared to allow abortion in certain circumstances,
though most would be strongly against any suggestion of abortion on demand. This is perhaps more of a 'gut' reaction than
any closely argued response, an awareness that most issues in
life turn out to be varying shades of grey rather than black or
white, and that there are situations in which the possible harm
of not carrying out an abortion could outweigh all other considerations. Where the matter has been thoroughly aired, as for
example in some of the reports produced by the General
Synod's Board for Social Responsibility,[13] the conclusion is
always that the unborn fetus has the right to both respect and
protection as a potential human being, and theologically as one
who is destined to have an eternal relationship with God. What
is questioned is whether the 'pro-life' position, that the unborn
fetus should be viewed in exactly the same way as it would be
if it was a newborn baby, follows from this. The argument for a
different view is based partly on the readily observable way

that the fetus develops. The most significant stages in this development are at the end of the second week, when the so-called *primitive streak* makes its appearance and implantation in the uterine wall is complete; at the end of the eighth week, by which time brain activity may be detected; and around the twenty-fourth week, when the child could be capable of surviving outside the womb. So, it is argued, that while the fetus has all the potential of a human person, it is not a 'person' in the early stages of pregnancy in the same sense that it is later on. This should alter the way we view it, and the degree of protection we afford it.

It is doubtful if these two positions can readily be resolved, at least on the basis of the physical facts. For while the fetus does develop in the way described, genetically everything is in place right from fertilization. So the 'pro-lifers' can argue that what you have is already a 'human being'. And so the two positions remain stuck at that point. The situation is not made any easier by the ambiguity of the terms used. 'Human being', 'person' on the one hand, and the impersonal 'fetus', 'embryo' on the other, have overtones which in many ways assume a particular approach before the argument has even begun. And once one gets into the realm of real controversy things get very much worse. The present pope's 'culture of death'[14] is the civilized side of the 'pro-life' lobby's calls to end what one *Information Pack*, which I have in my possession, described as a 'baby cull'![15] It is right that people should feel strongly on these matters, but the polarizing of positions and the intemperate language that often goes with it, are no help in resolving what for many doctors, priests and other carers, let alone those who come to them for help, is often a painful and confusing dilemma.

In many ways the real difference between these two positions lies in the way they approach ethical problems in general. The Roman Catholic approach is to identify certain general moral principles, which are seen as fixed and unalterable, and then apply them to specific situations. Others take the specific situation as their starting point and then ask what general moral principles are applicable. So in the case of the Roman Catholic Church the blanket prohibition of abortion rests on the general principle that human life is sacred and must not be sacrificed as a means to an end. That is fine as far as it goes, but it is not difficult to think of situations when this principle might well need modifying. Where a pregnancy poses a serious threat to the mother's life is an obvious example, and many would add others – the likelihood of the child being born with a serious handicap or malformation, or a pregnancy resulting from rape or incest. As Dr John Habgood has written:

A major difficulty in the attempt to derive clear moral deductions from general principles, is that the more specific the deductions the more controversial they are likely to be. Any move from the general to the particular entails an increasing dependence on the interpretation of empirical evidence the further one moves away from broad platitudes. Conclusions derived solely from general principles become more and more difficult to justify rationally without introducing all sorts of individual judgements, each of which may be disputed. In a nutshell the whole method runs the risk of trying to deduce too much from too little. In practice weak arguments presented to the faithful as if they were conclusive have generally had to be buttressed by an appeal to authority.[16]

Of course blanket prohibitions are attractive in that they are much easier to cope with than making individual judgements in particular cases. To say 'no' to everyone (or to say 'yes' for that matter), is much easier than helping an individual come to a responsible moral decision. But the question must be asked: Is it right? There will be situations when it will certainly appear that a blanket prohibition is both cruel and unfair, and abortion presents itself as the lesser of two evils. Those situations have to be catered for – though how they are catered for is another matter.

Abortion has become a deeply divisive issue in British society, though thankfully not (yet) as politicized and polarized as in the United States. When the matter is looked at coolly, however, from the point of view of the underlying theology, the real difference is seen to be not between the Churches, but between the Churches and those in our secular society who have a quite different view of what it means to be a human being, and especially those who because of this are calling for abortion on demand. Polly Toynbee's 'blob of an embryo'[17] sounds very different from the language of wonder and respect with which Christians and many doctors and others, who would not count themselves as believers, approach this whole question. I am reminded of some words of C.S. Lewis on the analogous subject of marriage and divorce. Speaking on the radio during the Second World War in some talks on *Christian Behaviour* he said:

The Churches ... all regard divorce as something like cutting up a living body, as a kind of surgical operation. Some of them think the operation so violent that it can't be done at all; others admit it as a desperate remedy in extreme cases. They are all agreed that it is more like having both your legs cut off than it is like dissolving a business partnership ... What they all disagree with is the modern view that it is a simple readjustment of partners, to be made whenever people feel they are no longer in love with one another, or when either of them falls in love with someone else.[18]

I find this analogy a helpful one, and the more so in that at the time it was made, the law was still maintaining the fiction that marriage was indissoluble and divorce was for hard cases, in spite of the way that public opinion was moving. Successive divorce laws have destroyed this fiction, and one can see the same sort of thing happening with abortion. The 1967 Act was designed originally for difficult cases, but it very rapidly came to be interpreted as allowing abortion on almost any grounds, and that is how things stand today. Christians are right to sound alarm bells about this, particularly when the pressure is beginning to mount for other changes in the law, notably over euthanasia. As Professor Robin Gill has written:

For my part, I worry that we might repeat the mistakes of the 1960s, which resulted in the Abortion Act. Then as now, there was considerable media pressure for a change in law based upon difficult cases. Yet, a liberty was soon turned into a licence... Could we be confident that a law allowing physician-assisted suicide, let alone more direct forms of euthanasia, would not follow a similar path? A liberty allowed on deeply compassionate grounds might then become a licence allowed on almost any grounds. The powerless, the depressed, the disabled and the vulnerable might soon become suitable cases for euthanasia. If we believe that life is finally God-given and that we should be particularly concerned about the plight of the marginalized and vulnerable, then I believe that we should proceed with real caution.[19]

These and other questions are not going to go away and Christians have an important part to play in determining the kind of society in which we live. In particular it is the 'side effects' of changes in the law which affect medical ethics, which have to be taken into account. Undoubtedly one of the effects of the abortion act has been to contribute to the devaluing of human life, and a relaxing of the law against euthanasia would accelerate this process. Indeed the British Medical Journal could argue quite recently: 'More, perhaps than any other, Britain is a post-religious society, where theological notions like the sanctity of life should not be overvalued.'[20] Christians need, in the words of the Roman Catholic bishops of England and Wales, to 'raise their voices'[21] against this trend, and not be seduced by the popular heresy that ethical and religious concerns belong to the private realm and individuals should be allowed complete freedom of choice in such matters.

It is interesting in this connection to see how a Marxist state handles such questions – in this case communist China. There we have the opposite extreme, with the common good taking precedence over everything else – in this instance the need to limit the population drastically so as to avoid famine. I remember a TV documentary on this, which featured a man and his wife who had started a second child. Considerable pressure was brought to bear on them to have the pregnancy terminated, starting with economic sanctions, and leading on to persistent visiting by the 'granny police' in the form of a middle-aged matron on a bicycle! In the end they capitulated, but not until the woman was eight months pregnant, when an abortion took place. It was a disturbing spectacle, but it did illustrate very clearly the mutual interplay between the values of the society in which you live and the respect for human life. We have a different problem in this country with the rights of individuals and their freedom of choice likely to dominate the picture, but this too can lead to a devaluing of human life through the opposite route of neglect of the common good.

All this is what one might call good 'headline grabbing' stuff, or what one Professor of General Practice once described to me as 'macro-ethics'. He went on to make the point that while matters like euthanasia, abortion, fertility, and experimental techniques raise huge problems and become a battlefield (or playground!) for theoreticians, philosophers, theologians and politicians, most doctors rarely come up against them. Consequently they often feel, from what they read, that medical ethics are esoteric. Certainly, the Ethics of Research Committee, with which I was involved for some ten years, rarely touched on anything so exciting or rarefied. Most of our concerns were with much more mundane matters – whether participants in a piece of research had had the consequences fully explained to them; whether it was clear to them that they would not be penalized if they refused to take part; whether a drug company was using this particular piece of research as a marketing ploy; or whether a questionnaire was likely to disadvantage staff through circumventing the official complaints procedure. Our concern was with what my professor friend would call 'micro-ethics', and this is what most doctors are concerned with as well. Included amongst these are the ethical problems which arise out of the doctor/patient relationship, and which are present in every consultation – such matters as respect, honesty and care. This is where 'patients' rights' come in. Essentially patients need the protection of 'micro-ethics' because of the imbalance of power between patient and doctor. The matter of power, and its use or abuse, is of course something which needs to be addressed by all professionals, including priests and ministers. The temptation to manipulate a situation because of your superior status or knowledge is an ever-present one. And other matters, of common concern to both professions, are important as well – for example, confidentiality, openness, and not hiding behind one's professionalism. This last, sometimes called 'the white coat syndrome' is not unknown amongst the clergy, and can be a real barrier to helpful relationships. I shall never forget the scorn with which a recently bereaved clergyman's wife described a visit from a minister that she had thought of as a friend. 'He tried to *counsel* me', she said!

All this takes us naturally to thoughts on clergy/doctor co-operation, for these sorts of issues, whether 'macro' or 'micro', need the expertise and insights of both professions. This is something which is very close to the heart of the Catholic approach to medicine, as is also collaboration in pastoral care at the grass roots level of parish priest and GP. Having worked closely with a practice in suburbia, which at one time openly declared itself to be a 'Christian' practice, I know the value of such collaboration. Sickness is a whole person problem, and most doctors (Christian or otherwise) are only too aware of sides of any given case which they are not trained to deal with professionally. So when a doctor says to a priest, 'Half my patients should be in your waiting room', he or she is expressing their inability to deal with what is often at the back of a person's illness – their inability to cope with life, guilt, an unhappy marriage, or some other spiritual or social problem, which the doctor feels ought to come within the priest's professional competence. Indeed it is a well-known fact that, particularly in suburbia where people feel themselves to be very much isolated units, they will seek out the professional that they know and trust and present the appropriate symptoms to him or her. Part of being a professional in such an area is being aware of this, so that talk of sleeplessness or headaches in the doctor's surgery, or difficulty with prayers in the vicar's study or the confessional, should lead to questions which uncover the real trouble and if necessary to referral to the appropriate person. Nor is this a matter for doctors and clergy alone. I remember a bank manager friend of mine telling me how many of his interviews with clients ended up on a pastoral level. What had started as a straightforward request for an overdraft rapidly turned into a discussion of something quite different – a marriage in difficulties, a problem teenager or a sick child. For this reason, if for no other, it is good when representatives of different professions can work together, and also meet together to discuss matters of mutual concern, and such doctor/clergy groups as exist demonstrate the value of this very clearly.

There are however difficulties, and this perhaps accounts for the frustration often experienced in trying to get such groups off the ground. Both doctors and clergy are usually very busy people, and making time for this kind of activity is difficult enough in itself. But there are more subtle factors relating to the nature of the two professions. A doctor's professionalism is based on an acquired body of knowledge and certain skills, the result of long training and experience. A priest's professionalism is similar in that he will have equipped himself through his theological and pastoral training to help people with certain problems, and he may also have developed other skills (such as counselling) which come from other professions. But there the resemblance ends. There is a whole side to a priest's ministry which does not fit into the professional model at all. The fact that he has been called by God to minister holy things to the people of God and to be their representative before him is something quite outside any categories of professionalism. It has to do with the 'Holy One in our midst' and his touch on the life of an individual, and it is something given rather than acquired. Many doctors of course understand this and respect it, but equally many do not and are suspicious of a profession which has this side to it. This is particularly true when it comes to the ministry of healing, for here those who are not doctors are beginning to trespass on what is specifically medical territory. It is here that the most damaging misunderstandings can arise, and so it is here perhaps that there is the greatest need for dialogue between the two professions.

Where the different roles have been recognized and brought together exciting developments can occur. Burrswood was an early example of this, with doctors, chaplains and lay people sharing in the work of healing, both in the house itself and in the services in the Church of Christ the Healer. More recently the hospice movement has demonstrated on a much wider scale the value of different disciplines working together, and the result has been to transform the way both doctors and many of the general public now regard the process of dying. A more recent development still can be seen in the willingness of some doctors to refer patients to Christian centres of healing. In 1996, for example, the Centre for Complementary Care near the West Coast of Cumbria, in which Christian healing was offered in the form of 'light touch' accompanied by counselling and prayer, actually negotiated a contract with the local Health Authority for a given number of referrals. This is a particularly interesting example, in that it was linked with a research project to monitor results, and this showed plainly that quite recognizable benefits in terms of pain relief, freedom from stress, and ability to cope were felt by the majority of patients who made use of the healing sessions.[21] The contract has not been renewed, largely owing to the tightness of the Health Authority's current budget, but local GP practices are continuing to make use of the Centre. Of course not all referrals of this kind have been to Christian centres. Some doctors fail to differentiate between the different forms of 'spiritual' healing on offer, but are ready to refer patients if they are convinced that they will be helped. And there is a growing acceptance within the medical profession of such techniques as acupuncture, aromatherapy and hypnotherapy. This raises other questions, but we shall be looking at these in later chapters. The positive side of it all is that there seems to be a growing openness on the part of the medical profession to the importance of spiritual factors in healing, and a willingness to follow this up in practice.

So we have come a long way since tragedy struck the Tait household in the 1850s. Had those children been born today they would have lived – though equally some of them probably would not have been born at all, because modern parents usually limit their families to two or three. But that too is evidence of the phenomenal success of medical science, that such limitation is necessary to prevent overpopulation. It is also a pointer to the new problems which arise, often out of success in dealing with the old ones – ethical and human problems as well as physical. All this has meant a revolution in the way we view health and sickness, a revolution which Christians have had to come to terms with, but out of it has come the revival of the ministry of healing which has been such a feature of Church life in this century. Meanwhile the scientific method itself, which has proved so highly successful as a tool in the development of this 'modern miracle', has been seen to have its 'flip' side, in that it encourages a culture in which people can all too easily become 'things' and their parts become more important than the whole. There has always been resistance to this, both in the medical world and the Church. However it is good to know that at the end of the century, there is this growing movement to treat people as whole persons, and that the spiritual side of men and women, as well as their mental and physical sides, is being taken seriously not only by the Church, but by many in the medical profession.

3 Signs and Wonders

'Miracles' and the ministry of healing

'How come you know Jesus and you no heal nobody?' A Sioux Indian Charismatic to a roomful of Roman Catholic priests.

(Francis MacNutt, *Healing*)[1]

ONE OF THE FASCINATING things about being a bishop involved in the ministry of healing is the way in which you can find yourself in a series of quite different worlds. One Saturday, I remember, it was a workshop on 'Saints for Healing', and anything went – miracles, slaying in the Spirit, demon possession. We even had a mention of blistered palms – blistered from the heat generated during the laying on of hands! Then on the following Tuesday it was London and a meeting about hospital chaplaincies with lots of 'NHS speke' and concerns about professionalism. Saturday's activities seemed a million miles away – in fact one bishop's adviser, I remember, even asked whether it would be wise for him to have anything to do with the healing advisory group in his diocese at all! And another spoke with some amusement of how a cathedral verger had sent for an ambulance when he saw people being 'slain in the Spirit' at a healing service there!

The fact that these different worlds exist, often in isolation from one another, accounts for at least some of the confusion and misunderstanding that there is in today's healing scene. To move from one to another is to experience a kind of culture shock. The language is different, the expectations are different, and the world view underlying what is said and done is different. And nowhere is this more apparent than over the matter of 'Signs and Wonders' – the whole 'miraculous' side to the ministry of healing, which is the subject matter of this chapter. The claim that miracles still happen is one which is widely made today, but equally one which is just as widely either rejected or only received with considerable caution. This is clearly something which is vital to one's whole understanding of any sort of ministry of healing – Catholic or otherwise. What are we to make of all the conflicting claims and attitudes which surround this particular subject?

To start with the claim that 'miracles still happen', there is no doubt that the high profile that the ministry of healing enjoys at the present time is due very largely to the Charismatic Movement – that dramatic upsurge of renewal, which started in the mid-1960s and spread rapidly through the main-line Churches in the 1970s and 1980s, and which its adherents likened to a new 'Pentecost', with its 'speaking in tongues' and other 'gifts' of the Spirit. As we have seen there had been a revival of the healing ministry early in this century, and this had had its quota of claims about 'miraculous' healings, but nothing on the scale of what was now being experienced by this new movement. Charismatics saw themselves as reliving the experiences of the early Church as recorded in the Acts of the Apostles, when 'signs and wonders' were a direct result of the outpouring of the Spirit at Pentecost and went hand in hand with the preaching of the 'good news'. As the 1981 Report for the General Synod on the Charismatic Movement in the Church of England puts it:

No amount of sterilization of the biblical message, and no amount of critical scholarship, have ever managed wholly to conceal the flow of the Acts narrative, and its message of a Spirit-filled community facing persecution, working miracles, rejoicing in the power of God, and generally living a corporate 'Pentecostal' life. The challenge is there – and the Church has always writhed slightly uneasily in trying to diminish the challenge. The alternative response – to rise to the

challenge and to attempt to live a comparable corporate life –
inevitably presses itself upon us. And the charismatic movement has
undoubtedly tried thus to rise to the challenge.[2]

And again on healing, which it too recognizes as having 'some
actual background in Anglican practice', it says:

However, the *mood* of healing in the Pentecostal tradition – the mood
which the Charismatic movement has exhibited and promoted within
the Church of England – could hardly be more polarized from previous practice than it is. Whatever the continuities with the previous
cautious and rational (though caring) ministry of healing, the dis-
continuities are far greater. The mood which has swept in is one of
expecting miracles. No longer does miraculous healing need explaining –
now it is non-healing which has to be explained! God is expected to
be at work in power, and the spate of charismatic books of recent
years fills to overflowing with the record of how God has both met
and exceeded these expectations.[3]

Since those words were written there has been no let up in the
spate of books produced or of the influence of the Charismatic
Movement. Healing services are now commonplace, whether
in the form of a regular offering of ministry Sunday by Sunday
as part of normal parish worship, as part of a large evangelistic
or healing crusade, or as a feature of one of the many centres for
healing which have also multiplied during the past decade and
a half. And there have been other developments too. Perhaps
the most significant has been the influence of the American
evangelist and church leader, the late John Wimber, with his
teaching on 'Power Evangelism' – that the proclamation of the
gospel must go hand in hand with God's revelation of himself
in signs, wonders, healings, miracles and Church growth. It is
these that convince people, he argues, rather than clever arguments, and he cites St Paul's experience:

In Athens, he had used persuasive words with meagre results. At his

next apostolic stop, Corinth, many believed. It appears that in
Corinth Paul combined proclamation with demonstration, as Christ
had done throughout his ministry. . . I call this type of ministry that
Paul had in Corinth power evangelism: a presentation of the gospel
that is rational but also transcends the rational. The explanation of
the gospel comes with a demonstration of God's power through
signs and wonders. It is a spontaneous, Spirit-inspired, empowered
presentation of the gospel. It is usually preceded and undergirded by
supernatural demonstrations of God's presence.[4]

Certainly for those who have taken part in John Wimber's con-
ferences there is no shortage of remarkable happenings. The
Revd Nigel Wright, a by no means uncritical participant,
describes what happened when John Wimber and his team visited his Baptist church in 1982. Following the prayer, 'Come,
Holy Spirit':

Within seconds the Spirit of God had fallen upon a large proportion
of the congregation, many of whom were trembling and shaking,
speaking in tongues, calling on the Lord, prophesying, and some of
whom (hard though it might seem to believe) were flapping up and
down like fish upon the floor. Some of this I was able to see, but most
of it passed me by since I was doing the same.[5]

He goes on:

It was our first experience of spiritual power in this way, and it
opened our eyes to the meaning of Pentecost. We could understand
why the first Christians could be accused of drunkenness. We began
to take with a new seriousness the dramatic encounters with God
that are recorded in Scripture and the strange phenomena which
would sometimes accompany them. The months following this event
were times of intense spiritual ministry, much of it in the area of
inner healing and deliverance.[6]

John Wimber's influence in this country has been widespread and has included such well-known figures as the late Canon David Watson and Bishop David Pytches. According to one writer who has made a close study of his methods,

since the mid-1980's, his involvement with British Christians has steadily extended, and now includes a 'network' of many denominations including what are commonly known as 'house churches'. Since 1988 Wimber has been establishing his own churches in the UK (called 'Vineyards'), and has also associated himself in leadership with churches and Christian leaders who aspire to the particular form of Christianity he espouses. Worldwide, Wimber supervises over five hundred churches.[7]

Over against all this enthusiasm and reawakening of faith in the miraculous, there have also been strong voices expressing caution and criticism. Some have simply been voices of disbelief, generally from the more Liberal wing of the Church and inevitably finding alternative explanations for phenomena which do not fit into their world view. But others, while clearly believing that healings do occur, are cautious or critical on different grounds. So Nigel Wright, who as we have seen has had first-hand experience of the Vineyard's 'signs and wonders', questions some of the more exaggerated claims made by John Wimber and his followers:

We cannot help but feel, with others, that the vast majority of claimed healings are in the area of the placebo effect. It must of course be conceded that just as sickness is complex, so is healing. A changed attitude to sickness is itself a form of healing. But it does not appear to be the case that there is much evidence for miraculous healing taking place such as we see in the ministry of Jesus and such as can be called 'signs of the kingdom'. The rhetoric about miraculous healing far exceeds the reality.[8]

Evidence for miracles is always difficult to assess, but it would appear that in some Charismatic circles enthusiasm does outrun the critical faculties. And this is given an additional impetus when 'signs and wonders' are required to provide support and proof of the authenticity of the message. There is a marked contrast here with the cautious approach to the miraculous exhibited by the Roman Catholic Church towards the healings at Lourdes, where every claimed miracle is subjected to close scrutiny over a longish period by an international medical bureau specially set up for the purpose. One of the last recorded miracles, for example, the disappearance of a leg tumour on an eleven-year-old Sicilian girl, took thirteen years before it was recognized as such. And in 1993 under the heading: 'A dose of reality for Lourdes miracle cure man' *The Independent* ran an article on a certain M. Charpentier which further emphasized this. In it, it described how M. Charpentier on his sixteenth visit to Lourdes regained the use of his legs having been a quadriplegic and confined to a wheelchair for many years. That was in 1988 and the medical bureau was still considering the evidence as to whether this was a miracle or not. Meanwhile the French Social Services had shown themselves far less sceptical than the Church and withdrawn his invalidity benefit![9]

How are we to assess all these conflicting claims about 'miraculous' healings? And perhaps more important how are we to assess what they actually mean or point to? Many of the criticisms of John Wimber, for example, are made not so much on the grounds that his claims were exaggerated, but that he distorted the Christian message by giving 'signs and wonders' too much prominence. How can we sift the true from the false here, and, if we come to some sort of decision, what will it all mean for our Christian Faith and the way we look at life in general?

In the end I decided that there was no substitute for a personal investigation of a particular case. So one day shortly after Easter last year, I caught the Intercity from Penrith to Crewe and went to visit Ada Hayward. I had first come across Ada in the early 1990s when I picked up her small booklet, which she had modestly entitled *The Meditations of a Channel of Healing*.[10] I had been taking a retreat for priests in Chester and the book was on a table in the entrance hall. At the time I was debating whether or not to give my usual address on a retreat as a 'healing experience', as I felt that I had 'run out of steam' on the subject. Her little booklet gave me the inspiration I needed and I went ahead. To add to the 'happy accident' aspect of it all, her vicar was on the retreat and I was able to talk to him about her and subsequently write thanking her for her help.

The particular incident that I wanted to talk over with her was one which she describes in her booklet and which was obviously of great importance to her. I reproduce it here with her permission:

About thirty years ago I was aware of something very deep inside me which I was not sure of but wanted to know more about. I was aware of lots of things happening but found I was not able to talk to anyone about it. At times I was very frightened and in a funny sort of way. What I did not realise was that I was experiencing the time of being shown that I possessed this gift of healing. Some people around me were aware of what I was capable, especially the Priest involved in that time of my life. He said one or two more could see what was being revealed more and more; they just knew and this proves how wise the living God is – I had a gift and it was to be used for His Glory.

One day my Priest came to see me. I was a busy Mum then with my children to look after and on that particular day had been washing, ironing, baking, sewing and generally working hard throughout my busy day. I was always glad to see him; he was a very strong Priest in every way. He told me he had come to ask me to do something for him which he knew I would take on happily. He said there was a young man who had met with an accident and, because of the head injury he had suffered when he fell, was rendered unconscious and had been in that state for a week or more. I was asked to pray for this young man. I was given his name and from then on that young man was, so to speak, on my shoulders. After a nice cup of tea and a freshly made cake, the Priest went on his way; like me he was a busy person.

Amongst other people I kept this young man close and prayed and at times fasted for him and the others. The weeks led into months and there was very little change in him; he was still unconscious.

My Priest came to see me again to tell me that he thought it was time for the young man to receive the Blessed Anointing and had made the necessary arrangements with his parents and with the hospital. I asked the time it was to take place and offered to fast and pray and give my support in this way. I told the Priest I would be in Church well before the time stated and would keep a vigil, fast and pray. I stayed up late the night before and did a lot of my housework; I baked and did all sorts of jobs when the children were safe in bed – my husband was a night worker so I was able to do this. I was making it possible for me to be free to undertake this act of love.

A little while before the Anointing was to take place I went to the little Church of St. Gabriel where I knelt and prayed. Myself and our living God, who knows us all, locked together in this wonderful love. Only the healing Power of Lord Jesus could help us now and whatever was to happen, would happen. The time drew near; I gave my Priest to Lord Jesus and told him what he was about to do. I asked Him to be there; I was very quiet and the Peace was so very deep. I was kneeling at the little altar, smothered in this peace and love and something strange happened to me; whatever it was came out of me in such force that I lost my balance. I did not understand what had happened to me but did not worry either, to me it was just one of those things.

There was an unusual rat, tat, tat, on the door at tea time – someone in a hurry – it was my Priest. 'Come on Ada' he said 'what happened to you in the Church? Are you all right, *were* you all right?' I asked him in and he told me what had happened at the hospital. At the appointed time he had ministered to the young man and, with the doctor and a nurse around the bed, did what he had to do.

Straight away and in such a manner it shocked them all, the young man woke up and began to talk as if he had never suffered unconsciousness for the last six months. He is alive to this day and leading a happy life.

I could not explain what had happened to me in the Church but told the Priest every detail. He said he knew something had happened to me and until he had been able to leave the hospital and get to me had been very concerned but in a faithful way.

After this event I was able to piece together a lot of things which, on their own, did not make sense but now they did and in depth too. I realised I had been used in this way for some considerable time but had kept it hidden; I just did not want to be 'undressed'; wanted it all to be hidden and was frightened – I just did not understand it at all in any way.[11]

I spent a happy morning with Ada. We sat in her 'quiet room' upstairs in the small modern house where she lives with her husband and talked about her ministry. In the room next door there is a bed that those who come to see her can rest on if they feel the need. Often they sleep and she keeps vigil over them. She exercises a quiet, hidden ministry fully supported by her parish priest, and always with reference to him. Much of what she does could be classed as 'inner healing', but quite frequently there are physical consequences. I noticed in particular that she seems to have a striking gift of 'discernment', often seeing pictures which illuminate a situation. Also she is able to detect what she calls 'hot spots' as she lets her hands travel over the person before her without actually touching them. She then lays her hands on them for a while. 'The person cannot feel the hot spot, only my hands tell me to stay awhile.' One thing is very clear, and that is the most important. She is deeply devoted to the Lord Jesus, and sees herself simply as a channel for his healing love, and this in its turn comes out of a deep prayer life and devotion to the blessed sacrament.

As far as the particular incident described above is concerned, the first thing to be said about it is that it does seem to be a faithful account of what actually happened. Having spoken with both Ada and her present parish priest, Fr John Mackey, I could detect no trace of any exaggeration or 'writing up'. In fact the reality was if anything rather more colourful. The young man in question came to and let forth a stream of swear words! But as Ada said, 'That was him – and he needed to let it out if Jesus was to enter him'. Again, his healing did not result in any noticeable conversion or anything like that. He occasionally came to church and eventually married a widow who was a chapel-goer, after which he moved away. On the other hand something had happened to him which clearly had an effect. He introduced himself to Fr John as 'the parish miracle', and Ada maintains that he was aware that Jesus was in him, though often he didn't want to know. All in all I was impressed by the low-key way in which the story was presented and the reluctance to make 'spiritual capital' out of it.

So where does this lead us? In the first place to a number of simple facts which have to be taken on board whether we believe in miracles or not. The most significant of these is the timing. The young man's recovery happened at the time that he was anointed. It also happened at the time that Ada felt something 'come out of her' with such force that she lost her balance. It could be argued that this was coincidence, but it is not the most obvious inference. Certainly that was not how it struck those who were there. Then there is the medical evidence. This is more difficult to assess as it is no longer possible to ask the sort of questions one would like to: Had the young man shown any signs of recovery up to that point, etc., etc.? One thing is clear though, everyone was very surprised at what happened, and his recovery (at least as far as his head injury went) seems to have been complete. Then there is Ada's experience while she was praying. In some ways this could be said to be more subjective, except that again it was clearly unexpected, and that she was literally 'knocked sideways' by it. I asked her what happened and she said that she had to grab the altar rail to stop herself falling. Whatever it was it had an unmistakeable physical effect of a quite forceful kind.

These, as I say, are facts and as such have to be taken on board. What we make of them will of course depend very much on our other beliefs. What I feel personally that I am not now at liberty to do, having talked with Ada and others, is to challenge the accuracy of them – to put them down to exaggeration, wish fulfilment, or 'writing up'. Of course if they don't square with your beliefs then you have to find another explanation. And there is just enough ambiguity in this story, as in most accounts of healings, to make this possible. 'I must have made a mistake in analysing the data', was a surgeon's response to the disappearance of a brain tumour, and that in spite of the fact that a bed had been allocated to the patient concerned and a date set for an operation. Her friends saw it differently. They had been praying fervently that she would be spared this life-threatening surgery. But he could have made a mistake. Surgeons know that they are not as infallible as the world sometimes thinks they are. And it could have been coincidence or some other natural explanation that caused that young man in Ada's story to wake up at that moment. It just doesn't look very likely to the unbiased observer. As has been said by more than one person: 'When I stop praying, the coincidences stop happening'.

I myself believe that we have to make room for 'miracles' in our thinking, as indeed we do for the activity of God in our world in all sorts of other ways. Even when full account has been taken of exaggeration and wishful thinking, I believe that there is enough solid evidence from stories like the one I have recounted at length (and there are plenty like it) to make one at least accept the possibility of 'miracles'. Of course 'miracle' is a slippery word, and if you take it to mean something that is totally against all known natural laws, you restrict it very considerably. But if, as with so many 'miracles' of healing, what it seems to mean is a miraculous speeding up or activation of the body's natural healing activity, it becomes a much broader concept and much easier to accept. We shall be looking at what constitutes a 'miracle' in more detail later, but for the time being Jennifer Rees Larcombe's definition is as good as any: 'A miracle is God doing something for us that we could not do for ourselves and another human being could not do for us'.[12] And she should know. For eight years she suffered from a chronic disease of the central nervous system and was largely confined to a wheelchair. On 13 June 1990 she was healed suddenly and completely after she had been prayed for by a young mother who had only been a Christian for a few weeks.

What about the scientific assessment of all this? Science in general has changed greatly since the days when it seemed to be on a perpetual collision course with religion, and it can no longer be said on *scientific* grounds that such things cannot happen. There are of course still plenty of scientists around who would argue that there is no need of a God to explain the phenomenon of our universe, but equally there are many who see in the way the universe is formed and functions many pointers to God's existence. The well-known picture of a group of scientists toiling up the mountainside of reality with ropes and ice axes only to find a party of theologians enjoying a picnic on the summit may be a complete caricature, but there is no doubt that science has moved a long way from the days when it saw everything in mechanistic terms. Modern science views the universe in a much more 'open' way than it used to, and has space now for such things as prayer and divine initiative to influence the way things are. As the scientist/theologian John Polkinghorne said in one of the Hockerill Lectures:

20th-century science has seen the death of a merely mechanical view of the world. In part, that is due to the cloudy fitfulness of quantum theory lurking at the atomic roots of the world. But it is also due to another unexpected insight of science gained in the last 30 or 40 years . . . Now, we've discovered that, in fact, almost all the everyday physical world is so exquisitely sensitive that the smallest disturbance produces quite uncontrollable and unpredictable consequences. This is the insight that is rather ineptly named chaotic dynamics. It came as a very great surprise to us . . . It is not altogether astonishing that the discovery was first made in relation to attempts to make models of the earth's weather systems. In the trade it is sometimes called the butterfly effect: that the great weather systems are so sensitive that a butterfly stirring the air with its wings in Beijing today will have consequences for the storm systems over London in a month's time. Now, that world is an intrinsically un-predictable world. We can't know about all those butterflies in Beijing. So we've learned that the physical world, whatever it is, certainly isn't mechanical, even at the everyday level. It is something more subtle and more supple . . . Such a physical world is one which, in my view, is capable also of being open to God's providential inter-action and his agency in the world. So that whole picture of the physical world has been loosened up. It is much more hospitable to the presence of both humanity and divine providence than would have seemed conceivable a hundred years ago.[13]

As far as medical science is concerned, one of the con-sequences of this change in attitude amongst scientists has been a new openness amongst doctors to the way in which the mind can affect the body. Recently there has been some solid research on certain aspects of this with surprising results. In particular the way in which states of mind together with major life events such as bereavement, divorce or loss of a job, affect the immune system has been carefully researched, and a link has been clear-ly established. In a lecture on the subject at the Middlesex Hospital in 1996 Professor David Metcalfe, a recently retired professor of General Practice, pointed to a study in Holland in 1985, in which it was shown that students' T cells[14] were reduced before exams. However in a group given relaxation exercises the reduction was significantly less. 'Work since then in disciplines ranging all the way from Anatomy to Psychology agree that the immune system responds to both nervous and hormonal signals from the brain.' When you realize that cancer is now generally accepted as being linked with a failure of the immune system, the importance of this conclusion cannot be underestimated. Indeed the original piece of research in Seattle at the end of the sixties and beginning of the seventies pointed to cancer as being linked to 'life events' as well as those diseases that we normally think of as stress-related such as coronaries and stomach ulcers. And if negative states of mind affect the immune system, so also can positive states, and in the direction of healing. That was certainly Professor David Metcalfe's conclusion: 'It seems to me possible that human interactions such as comforting, counselling and prayer can, by affecting the mental state, enhance the immune and other control, defence and repair systems'.[15] Again we are into that 'open universe' in which the mental and the spiritual can have physical consequences. And into something very different from past attitudes such as, for example, that a 'placebo' (a harmless pill which does nothing) or complementary medicine are to be welcomed, but only because they make a patient feel better. If they make him or her feel better this could actually have consequences to their immune system and contribute directly to their healing. To quote Professor David Metcalfe again: 'We have no excuse for continuing to think and behave as if mental states were irrelevant to the serious business of medicine'.[16]

All this seems a very long way from Ada and her deeply prayerful ministry, as it does from that of the many others like her. Yet in one sense it is not. It represents a convergence, and I find that very exciting. I do believe that it is important that the religious and scientific pictures of the world should at least begin to match up, and here is yet another example of science apparently enlarging its picture of the world in a way which supports religious experience. Religion is not meant to be about having to believe 'impossible things before breakfast'![17] Of course culturally these pictures *feel* quite different from each other, but that is not the point. What matters is what they actually represent, and what they represent is quite simply different ways of looking at what is increasingly being seen as one reality.

This leads on to the question of how God actually works, and here it is natural I suppose to draw a distinction between God's 'direct' action in answer to such things as prayer, and his working through 'normal' channels such as medical treatment and the body's built-in healing properties. Clearly there is a distinction, but is it just a matter of degree, or are the two different in kind? The argument so far would seem to point to the former, and certainly this is the way that fits in best with the sacramental approach to the creation, which Catholics have – seeing God at work in even the most ordinary of activities and not confined to a special compartment marked 'supernatural'. It also fits in with the way God so often seems to answer our prayers – not with some blinding flash of inspiration, but through some mundane happening. Of course people do have blinding flashes of inspiration, but even blinding flashes of inspiration are not God acting 'directly' in an absolute sense. Even the most 'direct' inspiration has to be filtered through our thought processes and the physical mechanisms which are our brains. That is why we are bidden to 'test the spirits' to see whether they are of God or whether they have somehow become distorted by our own interpretation of them.

The danger is always that we shall be so impressed by God's 'direct' actions that in the end we shall come to think of these as being the only ones that really 'count'. So, for example, Francis McNutt, in his well-known book *Healing*, ends his story of the visit of the three Sioux Indians with this comment (he is commenting on their claim that the Lord filled their teeth with silver fillings when they had toothache!):

The question, can it be true? confronts us all, as it did those 45 priests that evening. With most cures that we hear about we can imagine a natural process being speeded up; we often harbor a deep-down suspicion that perhaps a natural explanation can be found for what happens. But the filling of teeth? How can we visualize that?[18]

For me, that kind of comment sets alarm bells ringing. First of all, does knowing how something happens necessarily cut God out of the process? This is the old 'God of the gaps' scenario coming back again – limiting God's activity to those things which we can't explain. As everyone knows, the gaps continue to get smaller; and while it looks unlikely at the moment, who is to say that no one will ever find a scientific explanation even for miraculous tooth-filling, assuming that it actually happens? Of course there are different kinds of 'knowing', and it is here that science and religion most frequently find themselves in conflict. The scientific method is by nature 'reductionist', that is to say it seeks to analyze and reduce everything to its basic parts, whereas religion is more concerned with the whole, with its value, its purpose, its place in the scheme of things. Even if we know how something works that doesn't exhaust its possibilities. A sunset is more than the refraction of the sun's rays by the earth's atmosphere. It is a thing of beauty that can radiate peace and a gentle wonder at the day's end. So because we can see how some miracles might be due to the 'speeding up' of natural processes, that is not to say that God does not have a hand in it. His presence and activity are not dependent on our being unable to explain how a thing works. Once again we have to resist what seems to be an inborn tendency amongst some Christians to confine God to a compartment marked 'supernatural'.

This incident also raises the question of how far signs and wonders of this kind should be used to challenge people's ways of thinking. To be fair to Fr McNutt, he goes on immediately to pinpoint the question, which I suspect to many of the priests present was the real challenge: 'How come you know Jesus and you no heal nobody?' But the impact of the Sioux's claims about the healings they had received must have had an effect too. And there can be no doubt that God uses such confrontations to change people's lives. I can remember well the impact that Fr Jim Wilson's healing week had on some of the students at St Boniface College, Warminster back in the 1960s.

These were men who had spent the previous three years absorbing all the most up to date uncertainties from the biblical criticism of their day. And here they were suddenly faced with this deeply prayerful old prophet, who told them about things that they had long ago dismissed as belonging to a pre-scientific age. Of course some just shrugged it off. But the fact remained – either he was a liar, or ... !

We do however tread a knife edge here. As Nigel Wright has pointed out: 'There is a short step between knowing what it is to tremble when the Spirit comes and thinking that if we tremble the Spirit is bound to come'.[19] And the same is true of using 'signs and wonders' as a means of evangelism. It is clear from the Acts of the Apostles that signs and wonders followed and authenticated the preaching of the first Christians, but that is very different from saying that they used these deliberately as part of their mission strategy. In fact although on many occasions these seem to have been a powerful factor in bringing people to Christ, there are a number of incidents reported in which they had quite the wrong effect, as with Paul and Barnabas and the crippled man at Lystra. And certainly Jesus seems to have been motivated by quite different considerations in his ministry. From the very first he rejected the temptation to take short cuts with people by spectacular bits of magic like jumping off the temple pinnacle, and he refused to give the Pharisees the sign that they were asking for. He seems too to have frequently forbidden people to publicize the healings that they had received. All this should at least make us cautious about trying to use the healing ministry as part of any missionary strategy.

So what of John Wimber and his 'power evangelism'? All the cautions mentioned so far would seem to apply with particular force to his Vineyard ministries. By making 'signs and wonders' the central plank of their strategy, they limit God to a particular way of working, and that is always a dangerous thing to do. God does seem to work through 'signs and wonders', but he also seems to work through defeat and failure as well, and John Wimber and his followers have little room in their thinking for this. Of course it can be exciting and often effective to challenge the materialistic outlook of our Western world with happenings that collide head on with the prevailing world view, but it has its dangers as well. You have to deliver – and the accusations of exaggerated rhetoric and manipulation which have been levelled against John Wimber and his Vineyard ministries would seem to indicate that they sometimes have difficulties here. But what makes most of us uneasy is what their methods imply about God. In Bishop David Jenkins' words, our God is not 'a God of knock-down power', but a 'creative servant God of invincible love'.[20] John Wimber's fundamental error is that in the last analysis his way is actually the world's way of meeting force with force. As I say, that can be exciting, but at its best it can only be one side of the story. The God revealed by our Lord Jesus Christ is a very different God from that. He may at times show himself in works of power, just as at times he seems to overwhelm us with his love or with a sense of his presence. And these can be life- changing for the individual. But his greatest and most lasting victories seem to come when his 'strength is made perfect in weakness'[21] – as on that Friday noon outside Jerusalem all those years ago. We shall be looking at this 'mystery of success and failure' in more detail in later chapters, but it is fundamental to any discussion of the place of 'signs and wonders' in missionary strategy. What it means is that in the end neither the triumphalist approach of some Charismatics who put all their eggs in the 'signs and wonders' basket, nor the doctrinaire insistence of some Liberals that God *never* acts with power, actually does justice to Christian experience. There is a deep mystery about God's ways of working, and if we act as if this wasn't so, we are almost sure to get things wrong one way or another.

For my own part I would expect there to be a degree of ambiguity in even the most spectacular of miracles. This was even true of our Lord's 'mighty works' – not perhaps in the sense that they did not happen, but as to how they were seen and interpreted. The Religious Establishment of the day dismissed them as the work of the Devil, and we have a similar freedom. Again to quote Bishop David Jenkins: 'There is always a way of interpreting or explaining a 'miracle' which does not oblige anyone to attribute it to God ... God does not force himself on people. He offers himself to us for our response, obedience and collaboration.'[22] As Abraham said to the rich man in our Lord's parable (and this surely must assign even the most spectacular of 'miracles' to their proper place in the scheme of things): 'If they do not listen to Moses and the prophets they will pay no heed even if someone should rise from the dead'![23]

Not a lot has been said so far about specifically Catholic insights, though these certainly have a contribution to make to the debate about 'signs and wonders'. We have in fact noted one – the Catholic instinct that God is to be found in the normal as well as in the 'miraculous', and that to try to confine him to a compartment marked 'supernatural' is to ignore the sacramental nature of reality. That is a very important insight which underlies the whole Catholic approach to the ministry of healing. There are two other insights that we need to take note of as well.

The first is a matter of history. Until this century Catholics differed from the majority of Protestants over what they believed about miracles. Protestants believed that the age of miracles had ceased with the end of the Apostolic age, and used this as part of their anti-Roman propaganda when attacking such practices as prayers to the saints and the 'superstitions' that went with them. Catholics by contrast believed that miracles still continued in the Church, though admittedly only occasionally and spasmodically. They were usually associated with particular places and with the cult of individual saints, but belief in them remained very much alive as part of the tradition. All this changed radically in the latter half of this century, with the healing 'explosion' in the Protestant world, and the debate about miracles has now largely shifted to one between Liberals and the rest. One does however still hear echoes of the older debate, particularly in some Evangelical quarters. I have certainly found as much suspicion coming from Conservative Evangelicals as from Liberals, when I have talked about healing in clergy chapters. This stems mainly, I think, from a very proper concern about raising false hopes in vulnerable people, but sometimes, I suspect, there is also a fear that somehow or other it could lead to a watering down of Scripture. After all it is well known that most Liberals tend to dismiss the New Testament miracles as 'written up' examples of psychosomatic healings. So the need is felt to erect a ring fence around these to preserve the inerrancy of the Gospel narrative, and one way of doing this is to insist that Christ's miracles and those of the Apostles were different in kind from anything we know today. This is what the Evangelical doctor, Peter May, appears to be doing in an article that he wrote for Healing and Wholeness. The New Testament miracles, he writes:

included events which as far as we can understand have no possibility of carrying a natural explanation. The shrivelled hand, the kypho-scoliosed spine, the deaf-mute, the man born blind, Lazarus after four days in the tomb – all were healed instantaneously, completely and at a word of command.[24]

And he concludes:

We should pray ... for physicians, surgeons, nurses and others involved in patient care. We might also pray for breakthroughs in medical research. They are likely to be the main channels through which our prayers are answered. As for the laying on of hands, I find this has little warrant in Scripture. I feel we have made it into a mysterious ritual which is thought in our 'New Age' climate to have some therapeutic efficacy in itself. I don't think it has.[25]

Again the question must be asked: Is this a difference of degree or a difference in kind? Leaving aside the matter of whether or not any of the Gospel stories have grown in the telling, one would surely expect our Lord's healings to be more 'instantaneous' and 'complete' than ours. Even then he was limited in what he could do when he came up against the questioning and lack of faith in his home town of Nazareth.[26] This in itself should caution us against pushing the 'no natural explanation' argument too far. But the real flaw in this approach lies in its apparent failure to see that any sort of Christian healing is nothing if it is not *Christ's* healing. In Ada's words, those who practise the ministry of healing do so as 'channels' for Christ's healing. Of course they would be the first to admit that they are imperfect channels, but they are quite clear about who is doing the healing, if it happens through them. It is something which is quite fundamental to their spiritual experience. So the Roman Catholic Poor Clare, Sister Briege McKenna, speaks of her calling to engage in this ministry as being very much a personal one from Christ to her. Reading her story of how she tried to resist this by hiding behind her vows as a nun, and how eventually she was forced to accept it as a result of a number of different experiences, makes it unthinkable that she should see her ministry in any other way.[27] So whatever else can be said about healings today, it is not really a very good line of argument to say that they are different in *kind* from those of the New Testament. That is certainly not the testimony of those at whose hands they happen. They are clear enough that it is the living Christ who heals – the same Christ whose ministry we read about in the Gospels, active and at work in his world today.

The other fact to note is that for Catholics any ministry of healing will always be seen against the background of everything else that is happening within the Church. So it will tend to find its expression through those things that are central to Church life – the sacraments, prayer, holiness of life, individual vocation. Even when it erupts as part of a new movement, as it has with Charismatics within the different Churches of the Catholic tradition, the ongoing life of the Church is such that it can usually contain it, and at the same time keep it in proportion as being only part of a much larger whole. So there is a different 'feel', for example, about the ministry of someone like Sister Briege McKenna and Protestants like John Wimber and Morris Cerullo. 'I don't just roam around the world at random, simply because I think God told me to do so. I always tell my mother general what I think God is saying to me, but I am totally submissive to her decisions.'[28] This keeping of things in proportion is a particularly important consideration when it comes to the ministry of healing. This is the problem with movements like the Vineyard Ministries, devoted to a single strategic approach. Everything else gets subordinated to it, whereas in the larger institutional Churches there are always other movements to give balance to the whole. This is not a plea for the lowest common denominator or even for moderation. I believe that the late Canon Ernie Southcott was right when he said, as I heard him say on numerous occasions: 'That guy is one-eyed. But he sees a hell of a lot more with his one eye than most of us see with two!' It is the nature of movements to be 'one-eyed' and therein lies their challenge and their effectiveness. But they need to be balanced by other equally 'one-eyed' movements and contained within a whole. And this is where Churches as opposed to Sects always have the edge. They alone can hope to present a Christian Faith which is sufficiently balanced and rounded to serve the world as it actually is, with all its complexities and all its many differences.

So we come back to where we began with our different worlds, our different cultures, in today's healing scene. The danger is always that these will continue to live as if the others did not exist, or, if they acknowledge their existence, confine their activities to sniping at each other from behind prepared positions. I believe that it is important that they should meet and that they should engage with one another at a deep level. And this surely is what it ought to mean to belong to a Church which is truly Catholic, whether it be Anglican or Roman or anything else. There ought to be room within it for several worlds, several different cultures, and they ought to be learning from each other. Certainly God's healing activity is bigger than any of them.

4 Ask and You Shall Receive

Praying for healing

'Petitionary prayers ... are the right starting point ... They raise all the problems.'

(C. S. Lewis, *Prayer: Letters to Malcolm*)[1]

I AM TOLD THAT that great master of prayer, Archbishop Anthony Bloom, was once asked on television why it was so difficult to teach young people to pray. He astounded his questioner and others present by replying that in fact it was not difficult at all. There is a sense in which prayer is natural to people, whether they are young or old. He then went on to point to something which we all know, but often don't realize because it is so much a part of the way that we operate as human beings, that all the time our minds are sending out signals – hopes, fears, wishes, regrets, thank-yous, expressions of wonder. What is needed for prayer to happen is for us to direct those signals to God.

This is a good starting point for a chapter on prayer for healing because it dispels some of the false mystique that can so easily surround prayer. Prayer is here represented as something very ordinary and quite natural to us as compared with the special and elitist thing that it is often imagined to be. It is part of being human. Of course it is also part of a life-long pilgrimage of learning to know and walk with that Other we call 'God', and this has well-charted stages on the road and certain well-tried techniques which we may or may not find helpful. Most books on prayer are about these. But the stages on the road are the same stages that are to be found with any developing relationship – lots of conversation at first, then a deeper communion with less and less need for words. And even the techniques have to do with our make up, with the way we function as human beings – learning to focus our thoughts, using our imagination to step into our inner world, bypassing conscious thought to touch our depths. We shall be looking at some of these so-called 'methods of prayer' shortly, but here the point to be stressed is that there is nothing very special about them. Prayer is part of what it means to be human, even in its more sophisticated manifestations.

So what of prayer for healing, and all that has been written about that? Perhaps the best way into this much discussed subject is to start with a specific example and see where it leads.

A friend of mine told me how she and other members of her family had sat round her father's bedside in hospital. They had only been told the night before his operation that what they had thought were gallstones was in fact cancer. Now having been operated on he was barely conscious and the house doctor had said that he could not promise that he would last the night. His kidneys appeared to have packed in and it looked as if his coughing was keeping the wound open. In spite of this she felt very strongly that her father should live. She said it was like a religious experience – that God wanted her father to live because he had so much to sort out in his life, a great deal of grief, a great deal of pain arising out of the way his mother had ruled his life tyrannically. So she prayed that her father would have a year to sort his relationships out. 'It was an arrogant prayer and I really had no right to ask it, but I asked it nevertheless. Because we are encouraged to ask for things in faith.' And then she prayed bit by bit for the things that were wrong with him. She prayed that his kidneys wouldn't pack in, and he started to pass urine. And then she prayed that his coughing would stop and it did instantly. And by the morning they knew that he was going to get through the operation. Then the surgeon told them that they hadn't managed to cut all the

cancer away and that her father would be in a wheelchair within a few months. But that no longer worried her as she had
asked for a year. In fact he was still alive some nine years later
when she told me the story, and fitter than he had ever been,
with his colostomy reversed two years after his operation. And
some six months after coming out of hospital there had been a
different kind of healing. With the help of a neighbouring priest
he had managed to let go of all the anger and resentment that
had been there deep inside him for something like sixty years.
She said that the letting go meant that he cried solidly for three
days. But it opened him up to new kind of healing.

My first reaction, I remember, when I heard this story
was to be quite astonished as to how specific her prayers had
been. Praying that he would pass urine! And almost bargaining
with God to let him have one more year of his life. This of
course is in the best tradition of the Old Testament saints,
though I don't suppose my friend was thinking of Abraham
bargaining with God over Sodom at that particular time! She
just asked for what she felt was best for her father. But that in
itself is important. One of the great things about prayer for
healing is that it is so often earthed in a real life situation. So it
is real prayer – the very desperateness of the situation forcing
us to ask for what we really want, with no pretence and no
pious overtones. 'It was an arrogant prayer, and I really had no
right to ask it, but I asked it nevertheless.' But of course she was
encouraged to do so by our Lord's words about asking for
things in faith. Most of us know how easy it is for artificiality to
creep into our prayer life, what someone once described as the
feeling that 'you have to put on your best clothes' when you
pray. As so often, prayer for healing cuts right through all this
because it is dealing with real situations, real pain, real anxiety,
and we really care about the outcome. So experiencing something like this – or even just hearing about it – can have a transforming effect on the whole of our prayer life, rooting it in
reality – the 'real me' calling out in my need and helplessness.
This need to be yourself is something which the masters in

prayer stress again and again as a basic requirement. So Archbishop Anthony, in his famous 1950s' series of 'Epilogues' on *Prayer for Beginners*, gave his viewers as their first exercise the phrase, to be repeated nightly: 'Help me, O God, to put off all pretences and find my true self'.[2] And Sister Wendy Beckett in a book of meditations on art writes: 'Prayer is the only human action or state where cheating is impossible. As soon as pretence sets in, prayer stops.'[3]

This has important consequences when it comes to the sort of situations that leave individuals feeling angry and bitter. Angela Ashwin, who has written a number of books on prayer, tells of one friend whom she tried to help whose small grandson had just been diagnosed as having a fatal blood disease. 'I'm just so angry', her friend said. 'I don't seem able to find God at all.' Angela suggested that she might dare to make her anger an offering of prayer for the child, since this was the one thing she could give to God with all her heart at that moment. She also gave her a wooden 'holding cross' which she could literally hang on to when she could find no words for prayer. Angela went on to say:

She wrote later, describing how she had sat down and wept, telling God exactly what she thought of him. She had expected to feel ashamed for exploding to God like that, but she was surprised to find that her only sensation was one of exhaustion. Next day she felt that her praying had moved on, and she realised that she was being asked to stay there, in her misery, with God. 'It was like allowing a stream of pain to flow through me,' she wrote. 'I didn't resist it, and I held on to that cross. It made all the difference that God had let me shout and scream at him yesterday, and hadn't rejected me. Now I'm beginning to glimpse a bit of God's love again, though it's hard work hanging on to this.'[4]

Angela said that this letter reminded her of some words of Melvyn Matthews, who wrote, quoting Karl Rahner: '"Sometimes prayer is bleeding, as your sorrow trickles away silently", and its source the incompleteness of the human person.'[5] But the point here is that God accepts our incompleteness and our bleeding and meets it with love – indeed that is what the cross is all about. It is when we won't admit to our incompleteness in whatever form it shows itself, or try to bury it, that the healing and transforming power of God's love cannot touch us. That is why it is so important to be honest about our feelings before God. Those who wrote the psalms, the so-called 'cry of humanity to God', certainly never hid their feelings or allowed God to 'get off the hook'. I remember a friend of mine, whose wife had committed suicide, telling me how for weeks afterwards the only way that he could pray was in the words of the psalms. They alone expressed the bitterness and hurt that he was feeling towards God.

Of course not everyone reacts in this way, and certainly one of the signs of growth in the spiritual life is a deepening trust in God and the way in which he holds us in his hands. As a friend of mine once put it in a list that he had made of these 'signs of growth': 'Not badgering but trusting God'.[6] However a caution is needed here. Most of us don't come to such trust overnight, and sometimes there has to be a great deal of 'badgering' before we reach that point. This caution is particularly needed with prayer for healing, where it is fashionable to tack the phrase 'if it be thy will' or something similar on to the end of a prayer. It may be that we genuinely do not know what is best for the person concerned, but often we do, or think we do, and if we really care about them then we need to ask plainly for what we want. Can you, for example, imagine using such a phrase to the person's doctor? Indeed old Father Jim of the Guild of Health, for whom that particular phrase was 'anathema', used to say that it introduced a 'defeatist' element into our prayer and actually betrayed a lack of trust in God in that it showed a limited expectation as to what he could do. Be that as it may, the point is that there is no magic formula for learning to trust God. For most of us at any rate that quiet deep trust that 'all shall be well, and all shall be well, and all manner of thing shall be well'⁷ only comes at the end of a lot of striving and 'untrusting'. As Dietrich Bonhoeffer pointed out long ago in his *Cost of Discipleship*, in real life you cannot use the 'answer to the sum' as a 'formula' for living.⁸ You can only come to that answer, at least at any deep level, through the 'rough calculations' of experience.

What about methods of prayer? Not all prayer for healing comes out of crisis situations or involves people that we know well. Prayer groups in particular often have to fall back on 'methods', if they are to pray realistically for the list of names in front of them. And there are moments for most of us when our prayer goes dead on us and we have to fall back on particular techniques to see us through. Catholic Christians have a great advantage here in that they have a wealth of literature on the subject available to them, though, as was pointed out in the first chapter, other traditions are now sharing their own insights to the great enrichment of the whole.

The strange thing is, when you think of all that has been written on the subject of prayer, that our Lord himself had very little to say about prayer, and virtually nothing to say about 'methods' of prayer. And such teaching as he did give was almost all about petitionary prayer, the lowest rung on the spiritual ladder. That should make us hesitate before we attach too much importance to 'methods'. On the other hand he did have a great deal to say about the nature of God – in fact much of his actual teaching on prayer had to do with what God is like. I believe that this was deliberate. As C. S. Lewis says in the quote at the head of this chapter: 'Petitionary prayers ... are the right starting point ... They raise all the problems.' That is certainly true. If we ask God for something we are very quickly forced into all sorts of basic questions: 'What is God like?' 'Can he do what we are asking for?' 'Does he exist at all?' With the so-called higher forms of prayer on the other hand we can get away with something much vaguer. Indeed even atheists and agnostics can approve of such activities as 'contemplation' and 'meditation', ignoring their religious content and calling them 'relaxation' and 'reflection'. But with petitionary prayer you meet God head on, and there is no escape from those basic questions about who he is and what he can do.

So it is not surprising that our Lord's teaching on prayer has more to say about God than about prayer itself. And it is all summed up in that one word, 'Abba' – his title for God, in its original Aramaic a child's pet name for his father. Canon John Townroe, who has been a guide to so many through his long years as a spiritual director, says of this word that 'it is a word which invites us to approach God in a way which is:

simple,	bold,	secure,
direct,	obedient,	surrendered,
confident,	loving,	serene.[9]
intimate,		

What a recipe for our times of prayer, and particularly for those moments when we draw near to God with our own problems and the needs of others lying heavily upon us! There is a sense in which 'methods' pale into insignificance beside something like this. Yet, as has just been said, there are times when methods are needed, and they have their place. But as we use them we need always to remember that it is this loving 'Abba' that we are approaching, and that in the end that is what really matters.

There are two methods of prayer that I want to consider in detail, both of which in their different ways have a long tradition of Catholic spirituality behind them. The first is a form of prayer which has been variously described as 'contemplation', 'meditation', 'contemplative meditation' and 'affective prayer'. The names are confusing but behind them lies the very simple idea of opening the deepest part of oneself to God by putting the mind to sleep. This is most often done by the repetition of a phrase, of which the Jesus Prayer is the best-known example: 'Lord, Jesus Christ, Son of God, have mercy on me, a sinner'. Such phrases or words need to be carefully chosen if they are truly to express something of God's nature as revealed in Scripture and Christian experience, for this is a way of praying which is very much part of some Eastern religions and these have a very different concept of God. Our Lord's own name for God, 'Abba', 'Father', is an obvious starting point, and one that is not likely to lead one in the direction of Eastern ideas of 'absorption' into the divine. These phrases and words can also be used the other way round to express *our* longing for God, and this is important as the need is to 'know' him, rather than to 'know about' him. As the author of that great Western spiritual classic, *The Cloud of Unknowing,* writes: 'By love he can be caught and held, but by thinking never'. And he goes on to say: 'Strike that thick cloud of unknowing with the sharp dart of longing love, and on no account whatever think of giving up.'[10]

One of the best known adaptations of this method as a means of praying for healing is that made popular in the middle part of this century by Father Jim Wilson of the Guild of Health. Father Jim had himself been brought back to health in his forties, having been told that he would never work again, by this method of prayer, which in turn had been taught him by Miss Marion Dunlop of the Fellowship of Meditation. Basically it consists of repeating slowly a word or phrase which has been carefully chosen for its associations while sitting in a relaxed but attentive manner. 'Be still and know that I am peace within you', was one of Father Jim's favourites, and 'Lo, I am with you always, and that means now'. The idea was not to *think* about the meaning of the words, but to let them just sink down into one's depths, like dropping stones one by one into a well. There they would do their own healing work deep down in our unconscious, where all sorts of fears and memories lurk, and which normally we cannot reach. 'Words of life', Father Jim called them, but he was always at pains to stress the difference between what he was teaching and auto-suggestion. For the basis of his faith in this method was his belief that deep within each of us was God's Spirit, the Spirit of love and peace and joy and all those other things that we want and need for wholeness of body, mind and spirit. So prayer was not a matter of battering at God's door and asking for things, but of sitting quietly and realizing at the deepest level that in a sense we already possessed them.[11]

When it comes to using this method for intercession, for praying for other people, the technique is still the same. First to relax oneself – by consciously being aware of points of tension (a screwed up face for example), and then by slow and deep breathing. Then to repeat a phrase or word which opens you to God's presence and allows you to be a channel through which he can work. And then to bring the person themselves into the situation by repeating the phrase for them. I remember at St Boniface College, Warminster, how when the local vicar was in a critical condition following a heart attack, we all prayed for him with a phrase that was intended to enfold him in God's peace, which was his greatest need *physically* at that moment, as well as spiritually. In citing this example, however, it is important to note that the main focus must be on God rather than on the person concerned. Dwelling on symptoms in particular can introduce a negative element into the situation. In fact Father Jim used to tell of one prayer group that he had to tell to stop praying altogether, because their negative approach was actually harming those they were praying for. And when they stopped, some of those they had been praying for began to get better!

The second method that I want to consider is in marked contrast to this in that it seeks to reach one's depths not by bypassing the mind, but by using the imagination. As such it has affinities with Ignatian spirituality, especially as popularized by such modern writers as Gerard Hughes with his *God of Surprises*, and by the individually-guided retreat movement. It is linked with an observation by that great psychiatrist C. G. Jung, that when you use your imagination, for example by looking at a picture and trying to imagine yourself as part of the scene, 'the images have a life of their own and that the symbolic events develop according to their own logic – that is, of course, if your conscious reason does not interfere.'[12] And to illustrate this he told how a young patient of his had found himself walking in his imagination on the far side of a hill in a picture that he was looking at, and of how the images, which seemed to develop of their own accord, repeated themselves on a subsequent occasion.[13] This of course is a well-known way of meditating on the Scriptures – imagining yourself as part of one of the Gospel stories, a bystander or a disciple. What is perhaps not so often realized is that such imaginings can 'take off', and that when they do they can have important things to say to us, because they come from a part of us that is deeper than rational thought. Moreover God can use them as vehicles for communicating with us, just as he uses dreams and other more mundane means. Morton Kelsey, who has made an exhaustive study of all this in his book *The Other Side of Silence* speaks of our imagination as being 'one of the natural ways of getting into the spiritual realm'.

The key that unlocks the door to the inner world is imagination . . . Images give us a way of thinking that brings us closer to actual experiences of the spiritual world than any concept or merely verbal idea about that realm . . . When prayer and meditation concentrate only on concepts, they do not touch the most profound part of our being except when it happens accidentally.[14]

A striking example of the practical use of this method in praying for the sick is described by the General Secretary of the Guild of St Raphael, the Revd Michael Burden, in an article which he wrote for *Chrism*, the Guild's quarterly publication, entitled 'Creating an Inner Room':

I proceeded, in my imagination, to create a room deep within my soul where I could bring the sick, the suffering, the dying and indeed the dead before our living Saviour to receive his touch of life. The room I created was actually quite plain. At its centre is a fireplace,

with always a roaring fire. To the left is a door, and on the extreme
left a window which has curtains which are often drawn. There are
some pictures on the walls which I change from time to time, and
some plain and comfortable furniture. When I go to the room to pray,
I sit down and wait for a few minutes listening for a knock on the
door. Sometimes there is one, sometimes there isn't. Whatever happens I go to the door and open it, and Jesus is always there waiting
to come in. Sometimes he sits down, at other times he remains standing. Sometimes our discussion is about me – the problems I'm facing,
the mistakes I have made, the sins I have committed, and, most wonderfully, his forgiveness. But mostly it is about his willingness to
come to the help of those who I bring before him in need . . . What
happens is invariably unpredictable yet always moving. Sometimes
Jesus lays his hand on the person I've brought before him; at other
times they sit together and there is a discussion; at other times Jesus
puts his arms around the person and there is a time of hugging and
crying and peace. Whatever happens, as that person I know meets
with our Lord, so I bring before him also the names of the others
who are on my list [whom I don't know]. I trust that what I have
observed happening in my inner room with that one particular person, happens to each of them too.[15]

When it comes to methods, different individuals will
find them helpful according to their make up, but in the end
there is only one real rule to be followed. That is the much
quoted maxim of Dom Chapman: 'Pray as you can, and don't
try to pray as you can't'.[16] Some people are natural mystics;
others are down-to-earth practical types. For some 'meaning' is
all important; for others it is what you feel about a thing that
matters. Some get their main inspiration from within themselves; others from the world around them. And so on. With the
popularity of Myers-Briggs workshops many people now have
considerable insight into what makes them 'tick' as a person,
and this can be helpful when it comes to assessing the useful-
ness of a particular method of prayer.[17] But, as has been
stressed already, methods are 'good servants but bad masters'.

In the end it is the 'real you' praying in the way which is most natural to you at that moment, which is what matters. I remember how deflated I felt at the end of a parish retreat in which I had painstakingly described Father Jim's method of prayer, when the Charismatic vicar of the parish concerned said to me: 'We used to pray like that you know – trying to realize God's presence by repeating a verse from Scripture – but now the Holy Spirit just comes bubbling up from inside us!'

One matter which inevitably crops up when prayer for healing is being discussed is the matter of 'answers'. Why are some people healed and others not? 'I don't know why God was so good to us', was my friend's comment after the incident described at the beginning of this chapter. And the dismay which followed David Watson's death, when so many were expecting him to be healed, reflects the other side of this. It is a question which sooner or later confronts everyone who has anything to do with the healing ministry, and there are no easy answers.

Some of course will look for easy answers. 'Satan murdered David Watson', was the verdict of one of John Wimber's lieutenants in a BBC interview shortly after his death. And Jennifer Rees Larcombe tells of the number of people who, after her healing, wanted to know what she had done 'to get it right'.

All I can do is to admit that I have no idea why God decided to heal me that afternoon after 8 years of constant pain and severe disablement. That of course is not what they want me to say, perhaps because many people seem to be convinced there must be a secret formula for healing and if only we could crack the code God would grant instant healing. Perhaps one of the unexpected disadvantages of sudden healing is to be mobbed by these spiritual detectives searching for clues among the most precious events of our lives. Probably the only valuable thing they will discover is that God has a disconcerting way of treating us all as individuals.[18]

There are of course 'pointers', especially when it is the

other way round and our prayers do not seem to have been answered. Francis McNutt lists eleven reasons why people are not healed in his book on Healing, which include such things as 'lack of faith', 'sin', 'not praying specifically', and 'refusal to see medicine as a way God heals'.[19] But pointers are a very different thing from answers. I once heard Russ Parker, of the Acorn Christian Healing Trust, say how if you embarked on a healing ministry you would certainly see more healings, but you would also know more pain and more weakness – especially the pain of disappointment when healing did not happen, and the sense of powerlessness in the face of requests for healing. And he went on to say that no matter how often your prayers might have been answered in the past, every time you were faced by a new request, it felt like the first time.

There is also the further point that always in the ministry of healing we are dealing with very vulnerable people. And if their hopes of healing have been dashed, they will be feeling more vulnerable still. To suggest to them for instance that it is their lack of faith that has caused this failure or some unrepented sin, can only increase their distress and be deeply damaging. As it is this may actually be part of the picture, and it may be something that they come to realize sooner or later of their own accord, but human beings are complicated creatures, and the wise pastor knows that he or she treads on eggshells here. So much damage has been done to people by suggestions of this kind from individuals who must have everything cut and dried, that this cannot be stressed too strongly. We are not in an 'armchair' situation here, airily discussing interesting theories. We are dealing with real people, with real hopes and fears, and often in real pain.

So what now follows *are* only 'pointers', and I have selected what I think are two key ones, though there are others that we shall be looking at in later chapters. I suspect that they all contain a number of 'yes, buts', and I am sure that Jennifer Rees Larcombe's caution that 'God has a disconcerting way of treating us as individuals' needs to be borne in mind the whole time. Nevertheless they do shed some light on this mystery of why God seems sometimes to answer our prayers and sometimes not.

One pointer, or rather set of pointers, has to do with the whole area of belief, faith, expectations, whatever you like to call it. So we read that when Jesus visited his home town, 'he was unable to do any miracle there ... and he was astonished at their want of faith'.[20] I believe that occasionally there is a straight equation between lack of faith and failure to be healed, and this perhaps needs to be said. Generally, however, the picture is much more complicated. It is possible, for example, to believe at one level and not at a much deeper level. A key factor in this is the kind of society that we live in. In our secularized Western society we are surrounded by an atmosphere of unbelief. It is in the air we breathe, a lurking assumption behind many of the conversations that we have, and of course implicit in almost everything that we see or hear through the media. No wonder Christians find it hard to believe sometimes – really believe, that is, deep down. We are conditioned by the society in which we live to assume that such things as miracles simply don't happen. And it is our deep assumptions that matter, when it comes to praying for healing. I myself believe that one of the reasons why we have seen such a revival of the healing ministry in Charismatic circles, is that the initial Charismatic experience of being 'baptized in the Spirit' often brings about changes in a person at a deep level. Their expectations become quite different – enlarged – and this has its effect on their prayers, as well as on so much else.

We can of course help ourselves here. No sensible person engaged in the ministry of healing will attempt to 'go it alone'. If they are wise they will get together a group of friends to surround them and those they minister to with prayer and faith. And they will give time to their own prayer life, and to the building up of their relationship with God. There is a long tradition in Catholic and Orthodox circles of a link between healing and holiness of life. And one can see why. God can use those who are close to him in a way which he perhaps cannot use the rest of us.

Linked with this is what I call the 'desperation factor'. Just to talk about 'holiness of life' can trigger that off, if we are really honest with ourselves. We know that we can never be like, say, the late Mother Teresa, with her magic smile as she went about doing 'something beautiful for God'. It is magic, and there is no way we can manufacture it for ourselves. Yet this can have the effect of forcing us to rely on God in a new way, which is always a positive step in our growth as Christians. This is particularly so with those of us who are reasonably competent and self-confident sorts of people. We cruise along through life, paying lip-service to dependence on God – perhaps even preaching about it if we are priests – but in reality relying on our own resources and acting no differently from most other human beings. It is only when something comes along that we can't handle that we discover what it really means to rely on God. 'I thank God for this nervous breakdown' – so said a missionary to the psychiatrist Frank Lake. And he went on: 'For the first time I understand what Christianity is all about.' That was nonsense of course. But what he meant was that he had discovered the truth of what it means to depend on God in a new way and at a deeper level.[21]

This clearly has great relevance to prayer for healing. Because for most of us, such prayer whether it be for ourselves or for someone else is usually linked, as Russ Parker pointed out, with a sense of inadequacy and weakness. What matters is that we realize that this is actually a help with our praying, and don't try to run away from it. It is when we know that we are inadequate – really know that is – that we are most likely to throw ourselves on God in real dependence, and so our prayer becomes real prayer. I shall never forget kneeling in the chapel at Great Ormond Street Hospital after a visit to a goddaughter who was critically ill with leukemia. It had been a disastrous visit. I had hoped for a quiet and prayerful atmosphere as I laid hands on her, but the ward was very crowded and the little girl seeing her father behind me became very agitated and started to cry loudly for him. As I knelt in the chapel later, I remember praying: 'Not my poor prayers, Lord, but yours.' And then suddenly realizing at a quite new level what the phrase, 'through Jesus Christ our Lord', really meant.

The other pointer as to why our prayers for healing are not always answered is rather different. It has to do with that long tradition in both Catholic and Orthodox spirituality of the value of suffering – its *redemptive* value, both for the sufferer and possibly also for others. The modern Roman Catholic contemplative Thomas Merton sums up centuries of thinking when he says that no one can become holy without being plunged into the mystery of suffering.[22] This is not a particularly popular approach in our health obsessed society, but it is a good example of the way in which 'the tradition' can stand outside and so modify and correct the presuppositions of a particular time and place. Of course it must be received with caution, indeed with awe. We are on the edge of a great mystery here, and to assume lightly that God is calling one along this road can be a subtle form of defeatism, if not near to blasphemy. I myself believe that we should only reach this conclusion when we have exhausted every other possibility. It should be something that is almost forced on us; again, not a 'formula', but the 'answer' at the end of much agonizing.

I do however believe that God does sometimes say 'No' to our prayers for healing, because he has some deeper purpose in mind. Some deeper purpose for us possibly or for other people. Donald Nicholl in his book *Holiness* writes:

The worst thing that could happen to me in this life is that I should always have perfect health, always have interesting work and plenty of money to buy things and take holidays and also manage somehow never to be brought into contact with suffering. If that were to happen to me I should be turned into a monster, something unnatural, incapable of compassion for other creatures. To be cut off from suffering is automatically to be cut off from joy.[23]

In support of this, which he admits is 'the complete opposite of the answer that worldly folk give', he cites a number of examples of individuals who have been deepened and grown spiritually through their contact with suffering. So C. S. Lewis, that confident and popular apologist of the Christian Faith, could write after his new-found wife died of cancer: '[God] always knew that my temple was a house of cards. His only way of making me realize the fact was to knock it down.'[24]

This raises all kinds of questions and is certainly no answer to the problem of suffering, which remains a mystery whatever is said about it. But one of the shafts of light in the darkness is this perception, which so many people seem to have, that somehow and in some way this thing that has happened to them is 'for my own good'. 'It was terrible, but I wouldn't have missed it for the world' was how one person, who is very close to me, spoke of all that she had endured watching her parents slowly deteriorate before they died. And one finds that kind of thought echoed again and again.

When it comes to God having the good of others in mind we are into yet another dimension of this mystery. I think, for example, of a woman that I ministered to in hospital as a curate, who was a wonderful help to all those who were near her in the ward. I am quite sure that her influence would have been less – certainly quite different – had she not been ill like them. It was the fact that she was one of them that made all the difference. That is a fairly mundane example, but we can all think of people whose courage and cheerfulness in sickness or in coping with a handicap have encouraged and inspired all around them. Of course it would have been wonderful if they had been cured. But one can also see how God might have other things in mind for them, leading to a different 'good' and involving in some way the helping, even the 'redeeming' of those around.

That remarkable author and mystic Charles Williams once claimed that the true definition of Christ's Kingdom is to be found in the mocking words of those who had condemned Jesus to death: 'He saved others, but he cannot save himself'.[25] This, he says, sums up the relation of each of the Kingdom's citizens to his or her fellows. For we are indeed saved by others who cannot save themselves.[26] I think of occasions when individuals I have known to be most loving and effective pastors have come to me in deep personal distress. Moments like that are very humbling and make one very aware of one's own fallibility, and of how easily the roles might have been reversed. But they do more than that. They point beyond the immediate to that mysterious reversal of values by which God saves the world. It was when love bound him immobile on the Cross and he was unable to save himself, that Christ wrought his greatest healing – those hands that had healed so many, now stretched out in weakness. Here we see most clearly displayed that 'foolishness' of God, which St Paul speaks of, which turns failure and defeat into love's victory, and that 'weakness' of God which alone has power to change human beings from the inside.[27] I do believe that sometimes God does call us to share in his redeeming work in this way – in the way of 'foolishness' and 'weakness' – and that that can for some involve the 'failure' of not being cured, and the patient bearing of suffering or disability. 'That I may know him', writes St Paul, 'and the power of his resurrection, and the fellowship of his sufferings.'[28] Here is the heart of what it means to be a Christian disciple. To enter and share in this mystery of the 'weakness' and 'foolishness' of God in the resurrection faith that it is the means by which he saves the world.

There remains one aspect of prayer for healing, which we have not yet considered, and that is the very Catholic practice of asking the saints for their prayers. Recently I took part in a baptism in a Roman Catholic Church in which one of the names given to the little boy was Ciaran. Had he been a girl she would have been called Chiara, and Ciaran was chosen as being phonetically nearest to it. When I asked about this I was told that it was to St Chiara, better known in this country as

Clare of Assisi, that his parents had prayed when on holiday in Italy. They had been given little hope of having a child and attempts at fertility treatment had failed, so, as they told me, their prayers had been long and deep as they stood before her tomb. They felt too that they had a personal link with her as her feast day happened to fall on the same date as their wedding anniversary! Later, when they got back home, they discovered they were going to have a child, conceived while they were away.

I find the naturalness of this rather involved story quite disarming. Of course the practice of invoking the saints has been bedevilled down the ages by all kinds of superstitious practices, but here is a simple account of two people with a great disappointment hanging over them, asking for help from one whom they knew had been close to God in her lifetime and believed was close to him still. Many Anglicans are of course wary of the practice, and even if they are not, give the Church's teaching on the 'communion of saints' a very small place in their thinking and prayer life. I believe we are the poorer for it, missing out on what Archbishop Michael Ramsey once called 'a family unity of mutual prayer and thanksgiving'.[29] It is the awareness that we are not alone when we pray, particularly in times of crisis, which is such a help; that we can call upon our stronger brothers and sisters, who have trodden the same path of trial and suffering and won through, for the help of their prayers, just as we call upon our own friends who are still with us here on earth. 'The strong helping the weak', was how I once heard it described to me, and in many ways it is as simple as that.

For my own part, I must confess that prayer to the saints has never occupied a regular place in my prayer life. But my awareness of the reality of the communion of saints was wholly altered by two experiences that I had some seven or eight years ago. In October 1990 I went as part of a low-key delegation to the Greek Orthodox Church, which meant actually being shown a large number of their churches. And the first thing that you notice when you go into a Greek church is that it is full of *faces*. There in front of you on the iconostasis are the faces of the great saints, and all around you on the walls and even on the ceiling are icons and pictures of other saints – some well known, some known only in that locality. There is a sense in which heaven seems *to press in on you* in a Greek church, and that experience has left a lasting impression on me. I find myself much more aware now of the way in which we are 'surrounded' as we make our way through life – watched by those unseen multitudes, tier upon tier of them: 'Since we are surrounded by so great a cloud of witnesses, . . . let us run with perseverance the race that is set before us . . . '[30]

Then in the summer of 1991 I went into retreat on Bardsey Island, off the end of North Wales – the holiest of all the Welsh islands and burial ground of 20,000 Celtic saints. And that was to feel heaven pressing in on one in a different way – in the emptiness of sea and sky and mountainside; in the absence of man-made sounds – only the wind and the breakers and the cry of the birds. There is an old Celtic saying that 'Heaven lies a foot and a half above the height of a man',[31] and that was exactly how it felt – the sky so very close – heaven pressing in on one in that sense. It was on Bardsey Island that I met Sister Helen Mary, the elderly anchorite who had lived there for twenty years. 'Did you feel their presence', she asked me, ' when you were up there on the mountainside?' And when I had to say that actually, no, I hadn't been aware of the 20,000 saints in that way, she seemed genuinely surprised. And as I talked with her I realized that the saints of Bardsey were her daily companions, encouraging her in her life of solitary prayer. She even told me how this encouragement had once come in the form of their voices saying to her, as one hermit to another, 'We are the way'.

Here was someone who had chosen the solitary life, and yet never felt alone. And that is perhaps the aspect of the communion of saints which is the greatest help in times of sickness. Because when one is ill there are moments when one can feel terribly alone, and to know that you are 'surrounded' by that 'great multitude which no man could number'[32] and that you are upheld by their prayers can be a wonderful source of strength.

> O blest communion, fellowship divine!
> We feebly struggle, they in glory shine;
> Yet all are one in thee, for all are thine.
>   Alleluia![33]

This chapter has stressed the importance of being yourself when it comes to prayer for healing – whether you are calling on the saints for help, baring your soul before God, or falling back on some well-tried method of prayer when things go dead on you. It has also, I hope, stressed the other side of the partnership – the need for the *real* me to meet with the *real* God, and not some God of my imagining. In that series of 'Epilogues' already mentioned, Archbishop Anthony gave his viewers on the second week that he spoke to them the following phrase as their nightly exercise: 'Help me, O God, to discard all false pictures of thee, whatever the cost to my comfort.'[34] Part of the mystery of pain and suffering, at least as we encounter it in *real* situations, is that it helps us to do just that – face up to God as he really is. And that is the best start possible for any sort of prayer.

5 Thy Touch Has Still Its Ancient Power

The healing sacraments

'Sunday morning at five o'clock I heard the sweet-faced, gentle Catholic Fathers going softly from room to room on the promenade, blessing their people. I used to see them in the Bed-Rest Hospital and hear the soft murmur of their voices and even though I am an Episcopalian I often wished that one of them would stop at my bed, often thought that the Catholic Church alone has the true feeling of religion.'

(Betty MacDonald, *The Plague and I*)[1]

IN MY CHAPEL CORNER at home I have a small pebble which I sometimes use as an aid to meditation. It was given me by a friend who had been to the Holy Land and who had picked it up on the shore by the Sea of Galilee. Holding it in my hand when I pray, I find it works powerfully on my imagination – those feet would have trod on pebbles like this all those years ago, would have felt their smoothness and hardness underfoot. So I am led to a new awareness of the reality of the incarnation – of the reality of Jesus as a man of flesh and blood and bones who would have known what a pebble felt like when you stepped on it or held it in your hand.

What is really fascinating about this pebble, however, is that it not only stimulates my imagination, but in some mysterious way short-circuits the whole process and communicates with me direct. The feel of this smooth hard object in my hand – its realness, its solidity – speaks to me directly about the realness of Jesus as a human being. And it does so without any need for words – instantly and apparently bypassing the normal thinking process.

This chapter is concerned principally with the sacraments and healing, but any thinking about the sacraments must start with the significance of experiences like the one I have just described. Of course words play a very important part both in religion and in our daily lives – indeed we could not get along without them – but they are not by any means the only way in which we communicate and have things communicated to us. All the senses are involved in this. A smile or a touch of the hand can say more than words. A look can belie what someone has just said. A scent wafted on the evening breeze can evoke long-forgotten memories. Music can soothe or inflame according to its tempo. Silence can convey awkwardness or contentment and peace.

All this is commonplace enough but the sacraments begin with the commonplace – washing, eating and drinking, hands to bless and commission, love's commitment for life, a listening ear, soothing oil. It has been said that if you went to a desert island and couldn't speak a word of the language, the natives would still have some idea what you were about with most of the sacraments. There is a sense in which there is the same short-circuiting here as with the pebble from the Sea of Galilee. Of course sometimes the way the ritual has developed obscures the original meaning. There has not been much sign of *washing* in some of the baptisms I have attended, with something that looked like an egg cup placed in the font with only enough water in it to wet a finger! On the other hand to witness a baptism in a Baptist church is to experience a wholly new dimension – that of 'drowning' and 'resurrection' along the lines of St Paul's teaching in the Letter to the Romans.[2] Properly administered all the sacraments start with things that are familiar to us in our everyday lives, things which speak for themselves and at one level at any rate require no explanation.

At another level of course they do. For Christians see

these very ordinary things as being channels through which God's generosity is experienced. So baptism is an occasion for the washing out of the past and the beginning of a new life in the power of the Spirit; to receive communion is to be fed and nourished by the risen Lord himself; when we make our confession to another it is as if we made it to Jesus in the flesh, and it is from his lips that we hear the gracious words of forgiveness; and when 'the oil of gladness' soothes our brow it is Christ himself who stretches out his hand to heal. As the Dutch Catechism puts it: the sacraments 'are Christ's hands which now touch us and Christ's words which now ring in our ears.'[3]

From here it is a very short step to seeing other equally ordinary things as sacramental in the sense that they too have a deeper spiritual meaning – the world 'drenched with Deity' in C. S. Lewis's telling phrase.[4] Another 'sign of growth' on my friend's list (briefly mentioned in the previous chapter) was: 'Having a deepening sense of the mystery of life and of people'. Because we have discerned the presence and activity of God in certain special instances, so we begin to discern him in other things as well until the whole of life becomes 'an outward and visible sign' of the 'inward and spiritual'. Dr Martin Israel writes:

The usual worldly relationship is an I-It affair. When one speaks to another person, one is hardly aware of him as a distinct being in his own right, but simply as a sounding-board for one's own ideas and feelings. But when one becomes silent before the mystery of another human being (or animal, or plant, or inanimate object) and observes in wonder and respect, one is contemplating not only that person (or creature) but also God Who fashioned and created the creature.[5]

'Mystery' is a key word here, as are 'wonder' and 'respect'. One is reminded of St Benedict's instructions to his monks to treat their spades and other tools with as much reverence as the chalice.[6] And it has been said of the early Celtic Christians that for them 'nature was a kind of second sacred book, parallel to the scriptures, that revealed the divine'.[7] Here is a way of looking at life which continually penetrates below the surface of things and sees (in George Herbert's phrase) 'Heaven in ordinarie'.[8]

It will be apparent from what was said in Chapter 1 that this is a very Catholic way of looking at things. Protestants by and large do not feel so much at home with the non-verbal and the sacramental. As one writer has put it:

Protestantism is the religious expression of the print culture.
Protestantism arose and was shaped by the rise of literacy, the
explosion of books and the availability of the Scriptures made
possible by the invention of movable type in the century preceding
the Reformation. As a result, Protestantism has put so great an
emphasis on knowing God through the mind that it has sometimes
neglected or even denied knowing God in other ways.[9]

But Protestantism is changing as all living traditions do. It is certainly less dependent on the print culture, as that gives way, as it is doing in our Western society, to a post-literacy culture in which the visual reigns supreme. Evangelicals in particular have been very quick to make use of television and video and other related technologies as these have replaced the written and spoken word. And where the Charismatic Movement has had an impact the change has been even greater. Raised hands, clapping, and a general bodily 'letting go' in worship have been the outward signs of a new emphasis on the intuitive and emotional in religion as opposed to the cerebral – the 'Yin' taking over from the 'Yang'![10] Then there is the influence of the new religious culture 'out there', beyond the Churches – that of 'New Agers' and others. Here the thought that material things can be channels for the spiritual is commonplace, and the search is on for places and objects which transmit the right 'vibes'. While this does not usually carry much weight with the majority of churchgoers – indeed most Evangelicals would repudiate any idea that it did vehemently – it nevertheless is having its effect on the way people in general look at things. Ideas that would have been laughed out of court twenty or thirty years ago are now being taken seriously. The fact is that we now live in a climate, both secular and religious, in which the 'feel' of things, as opposed to rational explanation, is becoming increasingly important. 'Have you had a peak experience?' was the surprise question at a dinner party recently; not, 'What do you *think* about so-and-so?' – the question I have had so often in the past when people know that I am a clergyman!

I have dwelt on all this at length because I do believe that it is important that any thinking that is done about the sacraments should be against the background of real life as we experience it. What I have been trying to emphasize is that there is nothing artificial about the sacraments, but that they belong to the general way in which we experience reality. Physical things do speak to us direct, both about themselves and also about deeper realities. The sacraments are simply special instances of this.

When it come to specifics, the sacrament most closely connected with the ministry of healing is that of 'holy unction' or anointing. For those who are not familiar with this, what happens is that olive oil, which has been blessed by the bishop or by the priest himself, is applied to the forehead of the person concerned, the priest making the sign of the cross with his thumb, and praying over them. The form of words varies, that in the 1983 Order authorized by the General Synod of the Church of England being as follows:

N, I anoint you with oil in the name of our Lord Jesus Christ. May our heavenly Father make you whole in body and mind, and grant you the inward anointing of his Holy Spirit, the Spirit of strength and joy and peace.[11]

'Other similar words' are allowed by the rubric, and more elaborate forms are available in private collections and in services sponsored by healing organizations, and extempore prayer can also be used. It is generally assumed that the anointing will be accompanied by the laying on of hands, which in most rites takes place immediately beforehand, either in silence or with another form of words. Other parts of the body may also be anointed, most usually the palms of the hands. Anointing may take place privately as in a hospital ward, or in a public service. If it takes place in the Eucharist the 1983 Order places it just before the Peace, after the Prayers of Penitence. But practice varies, and a quite common arrangement is for the ministry of healing to follow communion or even to take place in a side chapel at the end of the service.

Holy unction has had a long and involved history. Olive oil was widely used as a medicine in Greek and Roman society. 'It was a universal salve – for sore feet, sore eyes, rough skin, broken skin. It could also be taken internally, based on the belief that internal pain was like external pain: an abrasion in need of soothing.'[12] It was also widely used as a medicine amongst the Jews of our Lord's day, as we can see from the story of the good Samaritan, in which he cleanses the traveller's wounds with wine and soothes them with oil.[13] It was natural therefore that the first Christians should use oil in connection with the healing ministry, and there are references to this in Mark 6:13 and in James 5:14-15. In the early Church the medicinal character of the oil still remained prominent, in that even when it was holy oil it was applied in much the same way as any other. There are a number of accounts of oil which had been blessed by a holy man or by the bishop being taken internally or rubbed on an afflicted area of the body; and the custom of taking it home for private application seems to have been widespread.

The evidence suggests that there was a good deal of 'do-it-yourself' anointing during this period. Phials of oil are passed from holy man to distressed woman, from monk-bishop to the terminally sick. From at least the third century onwards oil is brought by the people to the bishop for blessing; and it is taken home for use in any serious necessity.[14]

Gradually there came a change in the way anointing was seen and used. On the one hand it became formalized into a liturgical act performed by a priest, and at the same time it lost its purpose as a healing sacrament, at least in the West (the Eastern Churches have always retained this). So by the twelfth century it had become 'extreme unction', part of the 'last rites', whose purpose was to remove the last effects of sin (hence the anointing of the eyes, nose, mouth etc. – the organs of the senses). This change was undoubtedly linked with the way in which the Church itself changed once the age of persecution was over and Christianity became respectable. With the 'watering down' of the Church, healing became less and less part of the Christian experience. It seems too that St Jerome must bear some of the blame, in that his translation of the Scriptures, the Latin Vulgate and the only authorized text in the Roman Church for 1500 years, spiritualized the passage about anointing in James 5:14, and implied that it was about forgiveness and not healing. It was not until this century that the original purpose of the sacrament was restored (apart from a few brief instances), first amongst Anglicans in the 1920s and 1930s, and finally by the Roman Catholics with their rite for the Anointing of the Sick, authorized in 1974 as a result of Vatican II's directions on the subject.

A fourth-century hymn writer calls the oil used in anointing 'the dear friend of the Holy Spirit',[15] and the Syriac Church to which he belonged frequently spoke of Christ as 'the Wise Doctor, or Physician'.[16] Here is the clue to the meaning of this sacrament as it is now understood in most traditions. The outward anointing of the body with oil is seen as symbolizing the inward anointing of the person with the Holy Spirit, who is the agent of all healing whether of body, mind or spirit. And the anointing is done in the Name of the risen Christ, who is himself the 'Anointed One', the one upon whom the Spirit of God descended at the start of his ministry.[17] As Bishop Morris Maddocks has written: 'There is the conviction that it is being ministered by the Anointed One himself, the Christ, the "Chrismed"of God. In this sacrament we do indeed "hail . . . the Lord's anointed"'.[18]

Of course oil no longer has the same obvious medicinal associations that it had in the early days of the Church, but it can still speak to us very powerfully of healing and wellbeing. Its use in today's world gives rise to many associations of this kind. One has only to think of the way in which people cover their bodies with sun-tan oil, and then luxuriate in the warmth and feeling of relaxation which the sun's rays induce, to realize this. 'In Britain today . . . it would not be an exaggeration to talk about the massification of oils. They are used extensively and applied in a variety of ways, as bath oils, sun oils, massage oils, aromatherapy oils, incense oils, hair oils, and skin care oils.'[19] Quite apart from that the very texture of oil itself conveys the idea of soothing, of softening, of feeling good. There is a sensual side to the application of oil, it is 'touch-orientated', and generally linked with 'body loving' activities.

It is not perhaps surprising that one traditional Christian sacrament that has made an enormous come-back is oil: the most sensual, the most luxurious of the sacraments, and the one most associated with healing and making whole. Of all the sacraments, oil is the one that takes most account of our outward bodies. In keeping with this, many contemporary secular applications of oil, such as massage and aromatherapy, are aimed at uniting the body and mind by soothing both at once.[20]

If you ask, what is to be expected from this sacrament, the answer must be 'wholeness'. 'Give me the oil of gladness for wholeness' was the request of one hospice patient as the end drew near. His was an inner healing, one which enabled him to see his death 'as an adventure into the unknown realms of God's presence'.[21] But it can equally mean physical healing sometimes of a 'miraculous' kind. Bishop Morris Maddocks speaks of anointing setting off 'an explosive force in the person'.

Sometimes it separates the person from his disease, giving him freedom from pain and a consequent ability to live a normal life even though his body may still be ravaged by the effects of the disease. At other times it leads to a complete healing, for a time at least if not more permanently.[22]

He also speaks of a sense of forgiveness as being one of the 'bonus' effects of the sacrament, and says how many 'have witnessed to the amazing relief from the burden of sin which they experienced on receiving the anointing'.[23] All these are different aspects of 'wholeness', and there are others as well. Possible expectations as to what may result from this sacrament are perhaps best summed up in the prayer which follows immediately upon the Anointing in the American Episcopal *Book of Common Prayer* (1979):

As you are outwardly anointed with this holy oil, so may our heavenly Father grant you the inward anointing of the Holy Spirit. Of his great mercy may he forgive you your sins, release you from suffering, and restore you to wholeness and strength. May he deliver you from all evil, preserve you in all goodness, and bring you to everlasting life; through Jesus Christ our Lord. Amen.[24]

There seems to be a general assumption behind most of the modern rites that anointing will take place within the sacramental life of the Church, though it is nowhere stated that it is limited to communicants. The 1983 Order in the Church of England states that 'it should be used more sparingly than the laying on of hands, and is especially appropriate for use when a sick person is at a time of crisis.'[25] This is in accordance with Roman Catholic practice, that it is a sacrament for the faithful and that it is only administered during serious (though not necessarily life-threatening) illness. The laying on of hands by contrast is seen generally as something which is much more informal, though it may also be used as an alternative to anointing in a formal setting. Most modern orders limit the administration of anointing to a priest or deacon though some extend this to lay people authorized by the bishop.[26] And its administration is closely linked with the receiving of communion, and for those who wish it with confession and absolution. All in all the impression is that this is something for those who are in touch, or who can be brought back into touch, with the sacramental life of the Church.

The one exception to this would seem to be amongst Charismatic Evangelicals, where the practice of anointing has shown a remarkable revival in recent years. I have taken part in at least one evangelistic campaign in which coming forward for anointing was the centre piece of one of the evenings, and in which any one present was invited to come forward for this ministry. The authority for this practice is of course the mission of the disciples in Mark 6:13, when Jesus sent them out to preach and to heal, and it is recorded that they anointed sick people in the process. As yet there appears to have been nothing actually written explaining the rationale behind this practice, but a few enquiries have revealed a number of interesting features. Russ Parker of the Acorn Christian Healing Trust tells me that in the missions he conducts he usually invites people to come forward for 'the touch of God on their life in a new or renewing and revitalising way'. In other words the emphasis is not so much on healing a particular condition, as enabling the person concerned to move forward on their Christian journey, renewed and revitalised by the Holy Spirit. This fits in with the practice of the evangelist Eric Delve, who speaks of the oil of anointing as being for him 'a sign of the Holy Spirit, which is effective as real and as symbol'. And he goes on to say that 'when I anoint with oil, I believe that the Lord is in it, conveyed by faith and to be received by faith. I have therefore been willing to offer anointing as a sign of God's encouragement and presence to those attending a service for the renewal of baptismal vows and also to others who wish to be touched afresh with the presence of the Holy Spirit'. This interpretation also ties up with something that I was told by a parish priest, who has a regular weekly healing service in which he offers anointing once a month. He says that the Charismatic members of his congregation are happy to receive this ministry, and that they tell him that through it they have 'a sense of the Lord powerfully with them'. Eric Delve also has another interesting comment to make of a different kind. He says that 'one of the great advantages of using oil, is that, whereas the laying on of hands may well convey a sense of God's love and blessing and empowering at the time; after the event the hands are removed and the sign is gone. When someone is anointed with oil, they carry that sign home with them, and where the oil is perfumed, this can be a powerful reminder of the grace of God conveyed.'

What are we to make of this? My own feeling is that, whatever the tradition of the Church concerning anointing, this is a way of doing things which has clear scriptural backing. As such it deserves to be taken seriously as a legitimate departure from tradition, especially when it is remembered how varied the Church's tradition about anointing has been down the centuries. Moreover there *is* a tradition in the Church of anointing for service – in baptism, confirmation and ordination (not to mention coronation!). This practice brings this and healing together in a way which is entirely meaningful – healing for the past linked with prayer for a different sort of life in the future. While I have never used anointing in this way in an evangelistic setting, I have done so on other occasions – at the end of a retreat, as part of the preparation for ordination, and at an institution at the start of a new ministry. In each case I anointed the palms of the hands of those present as well as their foreheads, and the prayer was for 'the healing of all that hinders you in his service'. In the light of this experience I can quite understand why evangelists should want to use such a powerful sign of God's healing power in their missions. I can also understand why the practice has received such a ready acceptance, especially in Charismatic Evangelical circles. I do believe that it is something which we can learn from, even though we may wish to stay with our own tradition's way of doing things.

In focusing on anointing, it should not be forgotten that the other sacraments all have a healing dimension, for they are all encounters with the living Christ. Here the Eucharist occupies a special position, with the other sacraments forming a sort of 'cluster' around it. It is no accident that traditionally most sacraments are administered in a Eucharistic setting – bringing our particular needs to the feet of the risen Christ who is present sacramentally. Bishop Morris Maddocks goes so far as to call it '*the* healing sacrament'.

The Eucharist ... is a making present of Christ and his grace. As the liturgical action unfolds we are enfolded in the love of Christ, who makes himself known to us in the breaking of bread ... In the Eucharist the Church is absorbed into the joy and presence of its Lord, or, as Alexander Schmemann puts it, 'the Eucharist is the journey of the Church into the dimension of the Kingdom'.[27]

So the signs of the Kingdom may be expected to be present, and there is certainly some testimony that this is so. Francis MacNutt wrote as far back as 1975:

I know of at least half a dozen healings that have taken place during the Mass without any prayers being said other than those in the liturgical form; and I think I can say I have seen hundreds take place when I have added special prayers for healing after Communion or immediately after the Mass was over.[28]

And Sister Briege McKenna has a number of moving stories on the same subject. Most significant of all are her words to a young priest who phoned her because he was desperately worried about an operation he was to have for cancer of his voice box: 'Father, I can pray with you now on the phone, and I will, but this morning, didn't you meet with Jesus? Don't you meet with him every day?'[29]

John Gunstone echoes the same thought when he says: 'We don't just receive something but meet Someone'.[30] In fact there is more to it than that for the meeting is of a specially intimate kind – in particular the experience of touch is central to the Eucharist. We feel the wafer or piece of bread in our hands and then in our mouth, the cup as it is put to our lips, the sensation of swallowing. Sister Briege went on to say to that priest: 'Do you realize that Jesus is actually going down through your throat?'! While some of us might have reservations about this localized way of describing Christ's presence in the Eucharist, yet the sense of intimacy, of being actually touched by Christ, of his indwelling, is very much there. As we kneel at the altar rail it is the actual physical things that we do which draw our attention to the Eucharist as a healing experience. 'Dwell in me, as I in you.'[31] 'All who touched him were healed.'[32]

Thoughts about touch lead naturally to thoughts about the 'laying on of hands'. This is the most widely used of all outward forms of healing ministry, and can be seen to stem directly from the practice of Christ and the first Apostles as recorded in the Gospels and Acts. While it has never been given sacramental 'status' by the Church, it certainly 'partakes of the nature of a sacrament', with an obvious 'outward sign' and a corresponding 'inward and spiritual grace'. In practice its usage can vary greatly, from something that is little more than hand holding with prayer to a formal liturgical action akin to anointing.

The great advantage with the laying on of hands is that it requires little or no explanation. Whether it happens at a bedside or as the centre point in a large healing service, it is obvious what it is about. Touch speaks its own language and does not need to have its meaning spelt out. Even the link with Jesus can be implicit or simply made in the accompanying prayer. This makes it very suitable for ministry with those who are outside the institutional Church, or who have only tenuous links. As a priest has written, who has a special ministry with AIDS sufferers:

Touch tells [individuals] that they are still of value whatever their physical or mental condition. So often touch speaks louder than words. It restores a sense of value. It conveys unquestioning acceptance. It facilitates a release of emotional feelings. It communicates where words fail. It expresses concern and compassion. We should never underestimate the fact that touch is the simplest and most healing form of human contact.[33]

Gretchen Stevens, who practises a Christian ministry of healing at a Centre for Complementary Care in West Cumbria, says something similar when she describes how touch is so often the key that unlocks the door for healing:

I find that the first movement toward readjustment is physical. No amount of persuading, convincing or cajoling can release the tension that accompanies fear. The healing touch, slipping like a laser under the mind's defences can. When this connection is made, the spark ignited and the person *physically* and *actually* feels the shift of bodily emphasis, he can then mobilize his mental and psychological resources to help the body in its work of recovery. The touch which instigates this healing movement is very gentle, its effect powerful. Response in the first instance may be only a feeling of relaxation and heaviness. There may be sensations of heat or light, of vibration, of pulling of muscles. Tummies rumble. People sometimes feel they are floating or sinking. They may weep or sleep, talk or be quiet.[34]

This is to describe the natural effects of touch, but Gretchen's ministry comes out of a life undergirded with deep prayer. And while she in no way presses her Christian faith on her clients, her healing sessions with them are conducted against this background of meditation and recollection. So she goes on to say:

At this point people begin to feel better and sometimes mistake heal-ing for cure or partial cure of a specific condition. Healing is much more. We literally get more than we bargained for. I remember read-ing once that in early Christian apocryphal writing, Jesus is meant to have said: 'When you are near me you are near the fire'. I think that I have recognized that fire when I have seen the foundations of under-standing and belief of the most determined sceptics shaken as they feel the nearness of that Presence and Energy. Hands other than mine have touched them; they have gone beyond experience to a place new, which is also somehow home.[35]

'Hands other than mine have touched them' – that is the inward spiritual dimension to the laying on of hands. And it is in the faith that this is so, that his 'touch has still its ancient power',[36] that this ministry is so widely practised in today's Church. The Lord reaching out to those in need, as he did so often all those years ago.

However the very fact that this ministry has proved so acceptable to such a wide variety of groups in today's Church has its own problems. Certainly not every group finds the others' way of doing things acceptable at all. I find for example in the more Catholic Guild of St Raphael, whose magazine I edit, a very definite preference for a healing ministry that is low-key and sacramental and a marked distaste for 'up-beat' Charismatic services. Others feel differently, however, as I dis-covered when I organized a large healing service in Carlisle Cathedral in the cultural setting of cathedral worship (with motets sung by the choir and an *unamplified* music group!). While I found this deeply moving and prayerful, the Charismatics who were present made it very plain afterwards that they missed the informality and excitement of their own style of worship. So a number of questions need to be addressed, and not only the cultural ones, for culture and theology are inextricably mixed in today's healing scene.

It is quite common to make the sort of contrast which I have just made and see the healing ministry as divided into two camps – the 'charismatic' and the 'sacramental'. But that is really to oversimplify things. It is perhaps reasonably accurate to talk in this kind of way if one is only thinking about differing 'styles' of worship, and of course it is differences of 'style' which are the most obvious and the ones most people notice. However the picture begins to look rather more complicated when it comes to theology. Theologically Catholics and Charismatics are in some ways much closer than their differing styles of worship would suggest. For example, over against 'Liberal' thinking they both believe that God is active in his world well beyond what one might call 'normal channels', so that things like anointing and the laying on of hands do far more than just make people 'feel good'. And over against 'Evangelical' thinking both of them value physical actions as a means through which God can work, and see them as objective signs of his activity. So John Gunstone can describe the Charismatic experience of 'speaking in tongues' as a 'sacrament', and certainly it has the characteristics of one – an 'outward sign' of the Spirit at work.[37] It is perhaps not surprising therefore that the Charismatic Movement has found a place for itself within the Roman Catholic Church and amongst Catholic Anglicans. Or that when it takes root within Evangelicalism it radically alters some of the thinking and practice of that tradition.

One service that the Charismatic experience can bring to Catholics is to make the sacraments come alive for them in a new way. The words of the Metropolitan Ignatios of Latakia to the World Council of Churches Assembly at Uppsala in 1968 are relevant here:

> Without the Holy Spirit, God is far away,
> Christ stays in the past,
> the Gospel is a dead letter,
> the Church is simply an organization,
> authority is a matter of domination,
> mission a matter of propaganda,

the liturgy is no more than an evocation,
Christian living a slave morality.
     But in the Holy Spirit:
the cosmos is resurrected and groans with the birth pangs of
the Kingdom,
the risen Christ is there,
the Gospel is the power of life,
the Church shows forth the life of the Trinity,
authority is a liberating service,
mission is a Pentecost,
the liturgy is both memorial and anticipation, and
human action is deified.[38]

Formalism is always a problem for Catholics. Roman Catholics even have a word for those who regularly attend mass and receive communion without allowing it to interfere with their lives – they call such people 'over-sacramentalized'![39] It is easy to see how this can happen when the emphasis is on tradition and the Church's worship has become institutionalized. In Kenneth Leech's words: 'Religion ceases to mediate the world of the Spirit, and becomes a second-hand account of what was once experienced by people long since dead.'[40] On the other hand the experience of the Holy Spirit as alive and active in one's life can shift this focus from the past to the present. So the sacraments become real encounters with the living Christ. 'In my own baptism in the Spirit, on the day of my healing, the Eucharist took on a new meaning to me.'[41] So writes Sister Briege McKenna, and there are plenty of other testimonies to the same effect. As the Lutheran Carter Lindberg has commented:

The Charismatic contribution of raw and fresh primary religious experience is a needed reminder . . . of the fact that the Christian faith is not solely an intellectual enterprise . . . The charismatic renewal has the potential to recall us to Luther's own insights, into the depth, mystery and numinous character of the 'holy'.[42]

When it comes to what actually happens in healing services, we do need to be very careful not to let our personal likes
and dislikes colour our thinking. I realize that other people's
style of worship can be a very big 'turn-off', but I do believe that
it is important to try to understand why they find it so attractive, and to be objective about the pluses and minuses of different
styles. We are not all alike, and it matters that people be
allowed to worship in the way that best suits them and express-
es where they are on their spiritual pilgrimage. So I do not find
the sort of discussion you sometimes hear very helpful –
whether for example a quiet unemotional administration of
sacramental healing is 'better' than the heightened expectation
of a Charismatic gathering. Each has its place and equally each
has its dangers, and it is these positives and negatives that it is
important to focus on rather than one's own likes and dislikes.

When it comes to positives and negatives, the dangers
of the Charismatic way of doing things are well known.
Whipping up expectation can lead to a sense of let-down if it is
not fulfilled – one of the less desirable aspects of the tri-
umphalism which is so characteristic of the Movement.
Obsession with the sensational ('slaying in the Spirit', dramatic
physical healings) is a constant temptation for some
Charismatics – again the flip side of something good, the desire
for the power of the Spirit to be seen to be active and at work.
Then there is the danger that those with special gifts will
become the centre of personality cults, with the accompanying
temptations to manipulate people and misuse the power at
their disposal. And the emotionalism associated with some
Charismatic gatherings has its own dangers – a powerful agent
for healing in a controlled situation with experienced counsellors standing by, but potentially very destructive if help is not
available and where vulnerable and disturbed people are
involved.

It has to be said that many of those in positions of
leadership within the Charismatic Movement are only too well

aware of these dangers, and seek wherever possible to avert them. But these are real dangers and need to be taken seriously. They can do immense harm to individuals, especially if those individuals are already 'at risk' in other ways. As a friend of mine once said, when I asked him about the Movement at the time of my early contacts with it: 'It is strong stuff. If it goes right, it goes very right. But if it goes wrong, it goes very wrong.'

On the other hand, as has already been pointed out, most of these dangers represent the shadow side of the great positive truths that the Movement stands for – that God is active today in healing and renewal, that we should have a heightened expectation of what he can do, and that he does manifest himself in the 'gifts' that he bestows upon individuals through his Spirit. These are truths that certainly need to be proclaimed in spite of the accompanying dangers. I agree with Stephen Parsons when he says:

Although I have criticized some practitioners of this style of spirituality and healing practice on theological and practical grounds, it is in fact hard to imagine how Christian healing as a whole would have achieved its prominence in this last decade of the twentieth century without the important contribution of the charismatic style of spirituality.[43]

For those whose preference is for the more sacramental, meditative approach the dangers are all of the opposite kind – that the whole ministry will be so hedged about with safeguards (against raising expectations, against emotionalism, against any sort of personality cult) that it becomes a formal and to all intents and purposes 'Spirit-less' activity. The danger here is not that it is 'strong stuff', but very 'safe stuff'. It may not harm anyone, but how many will actually be healed as a result? I believe that Catholics always need to be on their guard against formalism. That is why alarm bells start ringing when I hear priests say things like: 'I always use a set formula when I give the laying on of hands. And I never allow "altar rail counselling".' For me part of the strength of modern Catholic worship and ministry is that it is so adaptable. It can include the informal without destroying the sacredness of what is being done or the sense of the numinous. So there is no need for this kind of restriction, which can all too easily turn into a 'stereotype' – the 'Catholic' as opposed to 'other' ways of doing things. I suspect this may be the reason why some of the more 'Catholic' healing services I have been to have had what I can only describe as an 'assembly line' feel about them. One longed for the ministry to be made in some way personal to those who came forward for healing, even if it meant prolonging the service – at the very least encouraging them to state briefly what they wanted this ministry for. Sickness is an intensely personal matter, often overshadowing everything else in an individual's life at the time, and this needs to be allowed for in any service that we arrange. So we must not be afraid of occasionally doing something uncharacteristic, or even taking the risk of being mistaken for some other sort of Christian, if this is the best way of really helping people!

All this of course is the shadow side of the Catholic concern to keep personalities out of things and focus on God's gift in the sacrament. As one writer has put it: 'We [must not] make our weak grasp of God more important than His strong grasp of us.'[44] And that is a vital truth that needs to be proclaimed strongly in the face of sensationalism and subjectivism. The great strength of the sacramental, meditative approach seems to me to lie in its emphasis that the healing ministry is a 'normal' ministry, something for every priest, for every congregation. As *The Book of Alternative Services of the Anglican Church of Canada* puts it: the laying on of hands and anointing 'provide the moment when the prayer of the Church for the healing power of God is made specific and particular in relation to this sick person.'[45] So it requires no special 'gifts' for it to take place – only reliance on the risen Lord, who blesses and heals through his Church, and whose loving ministry we encounter day by day in our prayers and in the sacraments.

Mention of 'special gifts' draws attention to what is undoubtedly one of the more difficult and controversial aspects of today's healing scene – the apparent existence of healing and other associated 'gifts' alongside the more 'normal' ministry of prayer and sacrament. What are these gifts and what are we to make of them? Are they to be encouraged or restrained? How important are they compared to the Church's 'normal' ministry? And what about those who appear to possess these gifts who are outside the Christian Church? Those are only some of the questions which they raise, and they are not easily answered.

It is perhaps best to start by trying to establish a few facts. First of all, to put it at its most basic, some people do seem to have a 'natural' gift of healing through their hands. This may not be linked with any philosophy or religious belief. They only know from experience that when they touch people they appear to be able to relieve pain and promote healing. Sometimes this is accompanied by the physical sensation of heat passing through their hands to the person that they are trying to help. Others experience trembling or something like an electric current passing through them. It would seem too that, whatever this gift is, it can be developed. Stephen Parsons tells of how his doorbell was rung one day by a woman who had just been to a 'healing' demonstration at a local centre:

The demonstrator had shown the participants how to focus their mental energies through their hands and she directed the group to practice on each other. My visitor found that even after this first demonstration, she was able to cause sensations of heat through laying her hands on her family members (though not her husband) and help them when they had aches and pains.[46]

Secondly there seems to be a close association between this and other 'gifts' such as the ability to 'sense things about people and places or to have 'premonitions' about the future.

Again to put it at its lowest, most of us have had unexplained 'feelings' about things from time to time, and these abilities would seem to be a development of this. In those who are psychically aware they can be very strong and uncannily accurate. I myself (who am not particularly psychically aware and therefore tend to be sceptical about such matters) have had more than enough examples come my way to be quite convinced that we are dealing here with something which is real. What exactly these 'gifts' are and where they come from may be a matter of speculation, but I am quite sure that they do exist.

I think it is important to start in this way with the phenomena themselves because in a sense it cuts them down to size. As we shall see, when we come to look at the deliverance ministry, there are some Christians who view all such manifestations outside the Christian Church as demonic, and because of this are almost paranoid about them. Conversely many of these same Christians appear to give an exaggerated importance to very similar gifts when exercised within the Christian fellowship. While not disputing the dangers that there may be when such gifts are linked with occult practices, or that alternatively they can become channels through which the Holy Spirit works powerfully, it is, I believe, important to see that in essence these are 'natural' gifts. That means that like all other natural gifts they are capable of being turned to good or evil uses.

My own feeling about 'spiritual gifts' as they are experienced within the Christian Church, is that the concept of being a *'channel'* for healing is a key one. That was Ada's phrase, and I believe it matches the experience of those who try to offer such gifts to God – that he uses their psychic openness as a way to reach out to people in need. In particular I believe that one of the reasons why the exercise of spiritual gifts plays such a prominent part in Charismatic ministry is that the Charismatic experience itself of 'baptism in the Holy Spirit' somehow opens up the psychic side of a person's nature, which up to that time is likely to have been dormant in today's cultural setting. Dr Martin Israel writes: 'I believe it is a psychic opening of a person who has been closed either intellectually or psychically; certainly it opens the psychic centres (of which the Church is very ignorant) for good or ill, and the power of the Spirit enters them.'[47] This is not in any way to denigrate the experience (though I am aware that Charismatics generally are suspicious of words like 'psychic'), only to seek to explain how the Holy Spirit may be working when it comes to the matter of spiritual gifts. As was said before, even the most 'direct' actions of the Holy Spirit are never direct in the absolute sense. Here he would seem to be using a mechanism which is part of our nat-ural make-up (though undeveloped in the majority of Westerners) in order to bring about healing when it is sought. The Charismatic experience is of course not the only experience which opens this particular door. There is a long tradition in the Church of it being linked with growth in prayer and holiness of life. The Curé d'Ars for example is credited with extraordinary insight in his dealing with penitents, and similar stories are told of many of the saints. This is the more traditionally Catholic way, and it is a sure way in that it puts the giving of oneself to God right at the centre of things, with such gifts as come one's way firmly on the periphery. To quote Dr Martin Israel again:

The gift of healing is in essence an ability to make rapid and deep soul-relationships – psychic empathy it could be called – with other people, and then becoming the channel through which the Holy Spirit can perform his renewing and sanctifying work. The mere psychic empathy will effect the transfer of spiritual power from one person to another, and some of those with a healing gift are neither believers in God nor especially admirable people. If they remain at a spiritually debased level they can progressively drain those around them, and in the end cause harm. This is why a gift of healing must be part of a deeper spirituality, one in which the person offers it, and indeed himself, unconditionally to God and to his fellow men.[48]

How do such gifts relate to the sacraments and to 'normal' ministry? The short answer is that they are both channels through which the Spirit works and therefore should not be seen as being in opposition to one another. The difference between them is that the sacraments are in John Gunstone's phrase 'covenanted means of grace', direct consequences of Christ's promise to 'be with us always', which have become generally recognized by the Church as channels through which his Spirit works. With spiritual gifts 'the grace has to be discerned in them'. But the distinction is to some extent artificial, especially if one takes on board what was said earlier about the whole of life being sacramental.

Both are acts of God through Christ among his people ... Christ's ministry can be interpreted both as foreshadowing the use of sacramental signs and also as a demonstration of spiritual gifts. If Christ is the Sacrament *par excellence* he is also the Charismatic *par excellence*. His ministry of teaching, prophecy, knowledge, wisdom, healing, deliverance and martyrdom, culminating on the cross, was charismatic-sacramental.[49]

That is fine as a definition, but in practice it can be very different. Those in authority have been by and large reluctant to give official recognition to those who have spiritual gifts, for example by licensing them as 'healers'. Dorothy Kerin seems to have been a partial exception here, but such exceptions have been few and far between. And it easy to see why. In real-life situations the eruption of grace can be a very threatening thing to those who derive their authority from the institution. The Sioux Indian's question is very pertinent here: 'How come you know Jesus and you no heal nobody?' The implication is all too plain – that in spite of your official position you don't really 'know Jesus' and therefore your authority is open to question. Small wonder that some bishops and priests react the way they do. Moreover, while this is a problem for all the institutional Churches, it is a particular one for Catholics. With their high doctrine of the priesthood, and their belief that ordination confers not only authority but a 'grace of orders' there is more at stake. The validity of the whole sacramental structure on which their ministry depends can seem to be under threat.

The only answer to this sort of situation is a return to basics. The only authority worth having in the Church is the authority which derives from Christ, and all in the end, sacraments, spiritual gifts and everything else, depends on him. So those who possess such gifts need continually to remind themselves that these derive from Christ and not from themselves. And those who do not possess them, need to remind themselves that Christ is not confined to one way of working, and that it may be his will to use them in other ways. And if the sight of 'spiritual gifts' in others leads those without them to throw themselves back on Christ that is all to the good. As we have seen, learning to depend on him can be very difficult for some people. The American priest, Robert Terwilliger, once said in a sermon:

I remember walking with a friend, who was in seminary with me, the day before his ordination. He had a seizure of common sense and did not want to be ordained. He knew that before him there was a vast unknown. There was something that he could not do. He was right. When we were given the Holy Spirit in ordination it was because we could not do it. If you feel inadequate to your ministry that is simply the truth. It is not we who are supposed to effect the ministry of Christ. It is Christ by the power of the Spirit that effects his ministry through us.[50]

Above all those with 'spiritual gifts' and those who have other gifts both need to remember that St Paul makes *love* the greatest of all gifts.[51] If that is taken seriously it is a very sobering thought. 'You will be judged according to your ability to love' – so writes Carlo Carretto, one of the Little Brothers of Charles de Foucauld, echoing St John of the Cross's famous words.[52] Love is something which cannot be manufactured, and as such inevitably throws us back on God. It can only be prayed for – and that is true of most of the things that really matter in our ministry.

'*Thy touch has still its ancient power.*' This has been a chapter which time and again has come back to a central theme – the presence and activity of the risen Christ *now*. In whatever way that presence and activity are experienced – through sacramental signs, through recognizable 'spiritual gifts', or through such everyday gestures as a touch of the hand or a smile – it is something which belongs to the present, to the reality of the here and now. So in all of these experiences we should look for the freshness, the sense of being on unknown territory, but also of total trust, which belong to a personal encounter with the risen Christ. As a Taizé letter, which came my way some years ago, put it:

The Spirit of the One who is Risen is always in you; he is never absent from your life. Knowing this is enough to keep us wakeful. And your night is transpierced by humble trusting in him.

6 What Have I Done to Deserve This?

Sickness and sin: healing and forgiveness

Whatsoever your sickness is, know you certainly, that it is God's visitation ... whether it be to try your patience for the example of others ... or else ... to correct and amend in you whatsoever doth offend the eyes of your heavenly Father.

(The Visitation of the Sick, *Book of Common Prayer*)

THEY WERE A SAD-LOOKING couple in their early fifties, and I noticed that he was wearing a round enamel badge on his lapel. I can't remember exactly what was written on it – *'AIDS a judgement?'*, something like that. But I know it was followed by the words, *'My God is not like that'*. Later, as we talked over coffee, I learnt that their son had died of AIDS.

AIDS makes a good starting point for a chapter which aims to explore the link between sickness and sin. Because of its close connection with promiscuity and drug abuse, it raises this question in its starkest possible form, and brings the different issues sharply into focus. Is AIDS a judgement of God on our permissive society? ... on homosexuals? ... on drug addicts? ... on particular individuals? Did God 'send' it? ... And what does it mean to talk about God 'sending' sickness anyway? Or is this way of looking at things totally wrong? What about Jesus' compassion for sinners? ... his care for the outcast? ... his condemnation of the hypocritical and self-righteous? And where does God's love come into the picture?

It also makes a good starting point because it brings out

people's 'gut reactions' as well. The Chief Constable of Manchester, James Anderton, caused a storm of protest when at a seminar on AIDS in 1986 he spoke of homosexuals, prostitutes and drug-addicts 'swirling in a cesspit of their own making'.[1] Yet in spite of almost universal condemnation from the Churches, the medical profession and agencies caring for AIDS sufferers, 'God's Cop' as his biographer styled him, received sackfuls of letters supporting his stance and only a handful of derogatory ones. And a poll conducted shortly after by London's LBC Radio produced a 74 per cent result in his favour.[2] On the other hand this has to be set against powerful feelings of a quite different kind, expressed for example by many of those who have been touched personally by the AIDS epidemic – friends, relatives, partners, carers. They see AIDS as something which awakens God's compassion rather than his condemnation, another opportunity for him to reach out to sufferers, and for us to reach out – 'My God is not like that!'

Dr John Habgood, the former Archbishop of York, commenting on these different reactions in an article for *The Times* in 1987, spoke about theology providing a 'framework of meaning' for our understanding the AIDS crisis:

Those who leap to condemn AIDS victims for moral enormities presuppose one kind of framework of meaning, one where retribution is writ large. Others who sit down silently beside the victims to bear part of their suffering with them presuppose another framework, one in which meaning is generated by compassion. The pragmatic 'technological' approach ('use a condom') sidesteps the question of meaning, but only at the cost of making the experience of the disease strictly meaningless, a matter of hanging on, hoping to be lucky, until the researchers come up with the answer.[3]

This idea of a 'framework of meaning' is a key one when it comes to exploring the link between sin and sickness. This is very clearly illustrated by the quotation from the Prayer Book Visitation of the Sick at the head of this chapter. This presupposes a framework in which God is seen as a loving but strict father, who does not 'spare the rod and spoil the child'. It also presupposes a pre-scientific framework – a view of the universe in which God is seen as directly controlling most of what happens, sending not only sickness, but determining the weather, the harvests, earthquakes and pretty well everything else in nature.

It hardly needs saying that these two frameworks – the theological and the scientific – affect one another. If we see God as being responsible directly for all that happens, then our first thought is likely to be: Why has he visited this particular illness on me at this particular time? If on the other hand we accept the normal scientific view that illness is caused by such things as viruses, we will ask a different set of questions: Who have I caught it off? Why did I let myself get run down? Why didn't I have that flu jab which the doctor suggested? We may of course then go on to ask ourselves what God is trying to say to us in this situation – that we should change our lifestyle perhaps, not work so hard, or cut down on our alcohol intake – but that is very different from saying that God actually 'sent' the illness in order to make us realize these things.

It is, I believe, no accident that by and large the fiercest condemnation of AIDS sufferers has come from the more fundamentalist end of the Christian spectrum. Theirs is a world view in which many things are still attributed to God's direct action, as this extract from a Church Society pamphlet, entitled *AIDS and the Judgment of God*, makes clear:

So far as individuals are concerned, Zechariah was struck dumb temporarily for his unbelief about the conception and birth of John the Baptist. Paul was blind for three days at his conversion. Elymas the sorcerer was struck blind for a time in Acts 13:11 and Ananias and Sapphira paid the ultimate penalty for their deceit (Acts 5:5 & 10).[4]

Here the authors of this pamphlet have no difficulty with the idea of God 'sending' sickness on individuals as a punishment, and never seem to ask the question, could there be another reason for it, which fits in more with the way we now view the workings of nature? Had they asked that question, they might have ended up with a very different view – a more compassionate one perhaps, certainly a more detached one which didn't find it necessary to bring God in in any direct sense at all.

How does God in fact act in relation to his universe? This, as John Habgood once said, is a 'tough' question.[5] But it is a vital one if we are to get our theological thinking about sin and sickness right. So, does God act directly on his universe in the way that many still think that he does? Does he, for example, as has been claimed, find parking places for harassed clergymen in answer to prayer, or washing machines for couples with no money starting a Christian community in their home? Alternatively does he leave his universe to run itself most of the time, only interrupting with an occasional miracle? Or does he not even do that, and work through 'normal channels' all the time, influencing events only through such things as the thoughts and choices of men and women, and the desire he has put into our hearts for a better world?

The short answer is of course that we do not know, and there is a sense in which each of these questions represents only part of the truth. Experience would seem to show that God does sometimes appear to lead people to empty parking places in answer to prayer, and it can feel like a miracle! But does he do it by miraculously reorganizing how people park on that particular day, or is it by something more mysterious – one of those strange coincidences which seem to happen in answer to prayer, or a 'feeling' to go down a certain street? It would also seem that things happen that look like a suspension of the laws of nature – healings, for example, when the opposite was predicted by the doctors. But are these really suspensions of natural laws, or are they more a speeding up of nature's own healing processes, or the harnessing of some latent power of which we are at present ignorant? We have already discussed this in some detail in Chapter 3, and came to the conclusion that the universe is certainly more 'open' to God's influence and activity than many would believe. We also saw that this has some support from the way much modern scientific thinking views the universe. Here what it is important to note is that all three of the views represented by our original questions are too simplistic. Christian experience would seem to point to a God who does answer prayer and does have some kind of direct input and control of events, and yet at the same time somehow allows his universe to run its ordered course.

As so often John Habgood brings clarity to this whole subject. In a write-up of a TV discussion which he had with a philosopher of religion, he said, 'I believe the answer [to the question of how God acts in the world] lies in asking how we act in the world'.

Though it is hard to describe exactly what we mean by it, most of us assume that by and large we are free agents. What we choose to do actually makes a difference to the way things are. Yet this free action takes place in a world, and through bodies and brains, which operate according to the ordinary laws of nature. We do not break the laws of nature every time we act freely or create something new. But neither do the laws, the regularities, say everything that is to be said about freedom and creativity. The universe, in other words, seems to be open-textured. Each of us know at least one place, in our own hearts and wills, where what happens is open to be influenced by personal decision.

If this is true of us, may it not also be true of God? What I am suggesting is that we should think of God as working through the regularities of nature in the same kind of way that we work through our bodies and brains. The fact that things *are* regular no more means that God isn't there, than the fact that someone has a reliable brain means that he isn't a person. And just as we sometimes reveal new depths in our personality by doing something unexpected, so God sometimes surprises us into a new understanding of himself by actions which, as it were, break the pattern. Whether they break it in some absolute sense, or whether they break only our inadequate grasp of the pattern, doesn't really matter. The point of such actions is not precisely how they happen, but what they reveal to us of God.[6]

What this means in practice, I think, both in relation to AIDS and indeed to other forms of sickness, is that we should look for natural explanations before we start looking for others. I myself believe that God does have a direct input into events and in various subtle ways does control them. That means that we cannot rule out that in some sense and on some occasions he does 'send' sickness, though if he does it can only be in accord with his nature as a loving Father who has a care for all his children. If we accept that our universe is such that he can work 'miracles' in it, then we have to accept that this is a possibility too. However I also believe that as a general rule this is the last explanation that we should look for, rather than the first. Generally it would seem to be much more a matter of God 'allowing' sickness, 'allowing' nature to take its course, 'allowing' on occasion our own foolishness and sin to bring its own disasters upon us. That seems to fit in much more with reality as we know it now, with the sort of 'openness' scientists and theologians are talking about in connection with the universe. As such it is a very different sort of 'openness' from that envisaged in the Prayer Book Visitation of the Sick, and a very different 'openness' from that of some modern-day fundamentalists who still see things in the Prayer Book way.

This leads on naturally to John Habgood's theological 'frameworks of meaning' and how they help us understand the way in which sin and sickness are linked. As we have seen there are at least two such frameworks on offer – one which majors on judgement and one which majors on compassion. There is also the framework, not yet mentioned which we shall be looking at more closely in the next chapter, which sees this world as the battleground between the forces of good and evil. And there is the framework of the secular world, which leaves

God out altogether and says very firmly 'no moralizing'.

I believe that a truly *Christian* framework (whether it leads to 'moralizing' or not) must always contain elements both of judgement and compassion. So the AIDS crisis should certainly make us ask questions about personal morality and the sort of society that we have become. In the same way the sight of starving children in Central Africa should make us ask questions about our personal acquisitiveness and our uncaringness as a nation. That is where the element of 'judgement' comes in. But side by side with that must go the element of compassion. That after all is what the Christian gospel is all about, God reaching out to us in compassion and love. And we have the wonderful example of our Lord's own ministry to remind us how central this is, and in particular, as far as AIDS is concerned, the way in which he so often sought out those whom the society of his day despised and ostracized. One of the questions sometimes asked of those who offer to help with work amongst AIDS sufferers is: 'Will it make any difference to you if the person you are trying to help is a haemophiliac as opposed to a member of the gay community?' It is an important question, for it is essentially a question about judgement and compassion. And it is very clear from the Gospels how Jesus would have answered it. He would not have skated over the differences between the two, but equally he would not have allowed it to get in the way of how he treated each of them. And if anyone had dared to stigmatize particular groups as being especially under God's judgement, he would have had some very powerful things to say about the dangers of hypocrisy and of being 'sure of one's own goodness'.[7] The Bishops of the London Diocese caught the feel of this very clearly in a letter which they sent to all their clergy in April 1987:

As Christians, our first responsibility to people who suffer from AIDS or who are infected with the AIDS virus is to give them the response we owe to anyone who is sick ... Furthermore, if we belong to Christ and are entrusted with a share in his ministry, this includes touching those whom society treats as untouchable, and embracing those whom society isolates.[8]

Finally there is the factual question as to what the actual link between sin and sickness is. Clearly there is a link, a very obvious one in the case of AIDS, but even with AIDS it is not as straightforward a one as some people think. If, as a member of a high-risk group, an individual engages in unprotected sex, he or she may well become infected. But equally they may be lucky, and innocent people such as haemophiliacs and the wives and babies of HIV positive men may be the ones who are infected. The connection is there, but it is uneven. This is something which needs to be taken on board, because it affects the way we see situations and individuals. And there are neutral factors as well. Air travel, for example, has contributed quite considerably to the spread of AIDS worldwide, and that must affect the way we look at things too. What is true of AIDS is true right across the board. As we shall see in Chapter 8, one of the biggest causes of ill health worldwide is poverty. Here there is a direct link between human greed and sickness. But the ones who suffer are the innocent. Once again the connection is there, but it is an uneven one. Human sinfulness certainly contributes massively to the misery of sickness and ill-health in our world, but more often than not it is the guilty who escape. And even when they do not, we should certainly hesitate before concluding that 'they have only got what they deserve'. It is very rare that we are in a position to know all the factors involved.

It is time we left the larger questions and focused on more practical matters. But the larger questions are important because they are always there in the background, and they affect the way individuals view their sickness and the way those of us who are pastors view it too. Individuals may not be able to articulate the 'framework of meaning' within which they try to understand what has happened to them, but it is none the less there and colours their thinking – sometimes in a very negative and potentially harmful way.

We should not be surprised, therefore, that, in spite of the widespread knowledge of what causes most diseases, many individuals still persist in looking for something in their past that would account for the fact that this has happened to *them*. 'What have I done to deserve this?' is a common question, as if there ought to be a direct link between the sort of person you are and the good or bad fortune that comes your way. My own feeling is that this is not a logical question, but one that express-es certain 'gut feelings' – that people 'shouldn't be allowed to get away with things' and that we 'bring things on ourselves', or on the other hand that 'life is against us' and that it is 'unfair'. These sort of statements need to be taken seriously in that they give the clue as to what the person is thinking and feeling at that moment. It is a well-known fact that the onset of sickness can bring out buried fears and feelings of guilt from the past. It can also bring out feelings of bitterness and anger at what appears to be the injustice of it. I remember my own mother, who had worn herself out caring for my grandmother, saying when she was ill in hospital a year or two later: 'You do your duty and this is what happens'. How many carers must have felt like that – and as we know only too well, caring for an elderly relative is a 'growth industry'. And of course it is no good pointing to the logic of the situation, that if you have an elderly relative to care for it is going to put a strain on you, and this may well lead to your being ill if you allow yourself to get run down. It *feels* unfair, and that is what matters to the person concerned.

Two things need to be said about these kinds of feel-ings. First of all there is a right and healthy sense of both guilt and anger, and it is important to remember this. There has been so much talk in recent years about morbid guilt, and about the need to be liberated from it, that it is often forgotten that both guilt and anger are natural reactions to certain situations and as such serve a very necessary purpose in life. Like pain they are signals that something is wrong, and like pain they are there fore essentially neutral. We ought to feel guilty if we have hurt someone or compromised our integrity, and we ought to feel angry at some injustice which has happened to us or someone else. If we don't there is something wrong, just as there would be something wrong if we felt no pain when we cut ourselves or hit our head. Having said that, however, we also have to recognize that guilt feelings and feelings of anger can easily go wrong. They can turn into an exaggerated sense of guilt which amounts to a moral sickness, or an underlying bitterness which colours the whole of life. Human beings are complicated creatures, and often the causes are buried deep in the past – an over-anxiety to please a disapproving parent perhaps, or a sense of injustice at the preference shown to a brother or sister. Whatever the cause it needs to be recognized that such feelings are definitely harmful and need to be healed. Not only are they harmful to the individual's personality and a hindrance to their growth towards maturity, they can also be mentally and physically harmful. As we saw in Chapter 2, it has now been clearly established that there can be a link between negative feelings and the immune system, so that helping someone to overcome their feelings of guilt or bitterness is not just a matter of making them 'feel better'. It may have important consequences for their actual physical health.

So what is to be done? The secular world offers a wide variety of treatments from pills to psychoanalysis. In particular in recent years it has provided opportunities to receive skilled counselling, and it is the growth of this discipline which has perhaps most affected the Church's approach to people with problems. Many Christian pastors have received training in counselling, and most are familiar with its basic tenets. There has also been a growth of 'Christian' counselling organizations, mainly from the more Evangelical end of the Christian spectrum. In general this more professional approach to people's problems is very much to be welcomed, though as we shall see it also has its limitations.

A simple illustration of how this more professional approach can help is to be found in the project known as

Christian Listeners, which Bishop Morris Maddocks asked Anne Long to develop for the Acorn Christian Healing Trust in 1985. This is a low-key project designed to help ordinary members of congregations to become better listeners, and in no sense sets out to produce professional counsellors. Nevertheless how we listen to someone – how we allow them to unburden themselves of their fears, guilt, anger, whatever it is that is troubling them, and how we ourselves react when they do – can make all the difference to the way in which they cope with life. The fact that such listening often happens in a quite spontaneous and informal situation, in contrast to counselling, makes it all the more valuable as a way of helping people when the listener knows what they are about. These extracts from one of the Acorn leaflets on the subject give a feel of this, and of the mixture of common sense and profound insights which have made these courses deservedly popular:

What prevents me from hearing others?
I am not listening when I am wanting to share my own experiences too quickly. I am not listening when I give advice before the other person has said all they need to say. I am not listening when I cannot stay with the other person's pain. I am not listening when I am too aware of feeling inadequate myself.

Practical tips for listening to others:
Listen to the words a person uses, but also listen to other parts as well: e.g. their faces, hands, gestures, silences, feelings. Don't interrupt. Don't offer explanations. Don't jump to conclusions. Don't put words in their mouths.
'The more you say, the less you hear.' (Joyce Huggett)
Ask God to help you focus on the person rather than on your thoughts and feelings.
      For a few minutes each day, try *to really* listen to your own spouse, a member of your family, or a neighbour – use the above tips. You will be giving them *a gift. You yourself will be a gift.*[9]

At the end of the day it is how you react emotionally that will matter most. Anne Long says that, 'We communicate our attitude to a person the moment he or she comes through the door'.[10] And this is very true. A nurse once described doctors as being of two sorts: 'Beside-the-bed doctors, who [are] interested in the patient, and foot-of-the-bed doctors, who [are] interested in the patient's condition'![11] It is simple things like that which communicate our true feelings, and we need to be aware of how significant even the most ordinary gestures can be.

Moving on to 'counselling' proper, what are its characteristics, and how does it fit in with normal pastoral care and such traditional disciplines as spiritual direction and confession? In the first place it equips the counsellor with certain professional skills, such as the listening skills outlined above, and provides training, usually in the form of casework which is undertaken under supervision. As a discipline it is essentially concerned with 'problem solving', and as such generally involves a series of fairly intensive sessions (possibly once a week) over a specific period. Counselling is also associated with certain values of which the most characteristic is that the counsellor should have a 'non-judgemental' attitude towards his or her client. With this goes an emphasis on building up a relationship of mutual trust between counsellor and client. The aim is to provide a safe and accepting environment in which clients are enabled to come to a greater self-awareness, and face those elements which are at the root of their trouble. 'Opening up' is how one counsellor has described the process, and he speaks of this as being at 'the heart of counselling – the opportunity and environment in which to open up and grow'.[12]

All this makes counselling a very useful tool, and it has certainly had a marked influence on how such traditional practices as spiritual direction and confession are now perceived. This is particularly true of its emphasis on being 'non-judgemental'. It is noticeable for example how nowadays the phrase 'spiritual director' is often followed by an apology, and an explanation that what is really meant is not 'direction' as such, but something more like the Celtic 'soul friend' – one who walks with you on your pilgrimage through life, and with whom you can share your experiences and your hopes and fears as you travel along together. The whole notion of being directive and of 'dishing out' advice, as opposed to helping people find their own solutions, has fallen out of favour, as has the emphasis generally on sin and repentance which was such a marked feature of the spirituality of former generations.

Not everyone has been happy with this, and there has been a suspicion particularly amongst some Evangelicals that the secular values associated with counselling are in some cases undermining the values of the gospel. Hence the rise of a number of 'Christian' counselling organizations, which attempt to engage in counselling within the framework of Christian beliefs and practice. Distinctive features include 'offering as a goal God-dependency as opposed to secular counselling's goal of self-confidence', 'allowing Christian values to permeate the counsellor, the relationship and the process', and 'making use of the spiritual resources of prayer, the Bible, the Holy Spirit as guide'.[13] Geoff Holmes, a counsellor from Gloucestershire, who conducted some research into some of these organizations in 1994, is critical of their approach in that it seems to be placing boundaries around the counselling process and in particular threatening the process of 'opening up', which is at the heart of counselling. In support he quotes from a book by Harry Dean, *Counselling in a Troubled Society*, which was influential in encouraging him in this research:

A great deal of formalized religion closes people down – and to that extent diminishes them – rather than opening them up, which is the task of counselling ... Religion can be so taught as to emphasise and confirm the deep inner subordination and stifled spontaneity of the vital heart of the personality.[14]

He concludes by saying that he 'would be happier to be a Christian who counsels rather than being in the pigeon-hole of a "Christian counsellor"'. But be that as it may, these organizations are certainly right, in that they clearly see that the 'framework of meaning' within which one approaches counselling is of first importance. That must affect one's whole way of working. It may be that in the eyes of people like Geoff Holmes their framework is too narrow, but that is a different matter. Whether you call yourself a 'Christian counsellor' or a 'Christian who counsels', you bring to your work certain beliefs and values and these are bound at times to call in question some of the beliefs and values behind secular counselling.

This is perhaps seen most clearly in the matter of 'goals'. We have already seen how some Christian counsellors contrast 'God-dependency' with self-reliance. There are question marks round this, in that there is a right and wrong sort of dependency, but in the end most spiritual writers would agree that living as a Christian does mean living in dependence on God, and that one of the signs of growth is the discovery of this for ourselves. Similarly Christians set their sights well beyond the counselling ideal of the 'well-adjusted' person. One secular writer for example defines counselling as 'a relationship in which one person endeavours to help another to understand and solve his difficulties of adjustment to society'.[15] This, as Kenneth Leech points out, is 'a highly dubious goal for a Christian',[16] and he quotes the American liberal writer, Daniel Day Williams:

The Christian ideal of life envisions something higher than freedom from anguish or invulnerability to its ravages. Its goal cannot be the perfectly adjusted self. In the world as it is, a caring love cannot but regard such a goal as intolerably self-centred. What does it mean to be completely adjusted and at peace in a world so riddled with injustice and the cries of the hungry, with the great unsolved questions of human living as this? We see why in the end we cannot identify therapy for specific ills with salvation for the human spirit. To live in love means to accept the risks of life and its threats to 'peace of mind'.[17]

This is to introduce the Catholic concept of 'sainthood', and indeed one cannot talk about 'goals' without talking about saints. For the Christian 'framework of meaning' speaks of a 'Christlike' God – a Love at the heart of the universe who continually gives himself to us, and calls for a 'Christlike' giving of ourselves in return. That and nothing less. Hence Archbishop Michael Ramsey's well-known saying that 'to be healthy and to be whole is no substitute for being penitent, forgiven and holy'.[18] That would be considered almost 'blasphemous' in some counselling circles. And possibly in some healing circles as well, where the word 'wholeness' has become a sort of sacred shibboleth! 'Wholeness' is of course an important word and a useful one in that it emphasizes that there is more to health than physical cure. But one cannot help feeling that the way in which it is sometimes used actually owes more to modern Western thinking than to Christian spirituality! The ideal of the balanced, mature, integrated personality is fine as far as it goes, but it does not begin to measure up to the Christian notion of sanctity. It is not the way in which one would, for example, describe St Francis, who for love's sake 'counted the wisdom of this world as foolishness' and in the process ruined his health and died in his forties. The world is not set on fire by balanced, mature, integrated personalities but by saints, by those who are prepared to give themselves in one way or another to a heroic following of Christ, for love of God and their fellow men and women. That is a very different ideal from Western man's 'sensible' ideal of maturity, and it is something that needs to be borne in mind whenever the word 'wholeness' is used.

What then is the relationship between penitence and healing and between forgiveness and healing? The two have always been seen to be linked in Catholic circles, where confession of sin has generally been expected as a preliminary to receiving anointing or the laying on of hands. And other Christian traditions emphasize the need to 'be right' with God in their own particular ways. So, as we have seen, Francis MacNutt, for example, lists 'sin' among his eleven reasons why some people are not healed in answer to prayer, and other Charismatic books on the subject take a similar line. That 'sin' is a blockage to prayer is so obvious as hardly to need stating, and any Christian seeking healing will do their best to 'get right' with God as part of their preparation for it. But of course things are not always as simple as that. Many people have blockages of a deeper kind – fears and resentments, buried anger, bitterness – which they cannot shed just like that. These things also need healing, and it is part of the ministry both of forgiveness and of healing to recognize that this is often the case.

Traditionally Catholics have sought help with this through the sacrament of penance – through confession to a priest and absolution. The Anglican tradition has always been to link this with advice and often too with spiritual direction, and this is now much more the Roman Catholic practice as well. Recently too confession has become more informal in both Churches, with a greater emphasis on the counselling element. I noticed, for example, a few years ago when I was in Paris that in Notre Dame, along with the traditional confessional boxes, there was also a small room with a table and two chairs set aside for an 'interview' style of confession. This is a healthy development insofar as it enables there to be discussion of problems at a greater depth. But it always needs to be remembered that at the end of the day confession is about laying your life before God and seeking his forgiveness for all that is wrong in it. Donald Nicholl in his book *Holiness* has some strong things to say about this. He writes of the need to take 'total responsibility for all that we *are* and not simply how we *appear* to other human beings'.[19] And he draws attention in particular to the *objective* nature of the sinful element in some of our actions and the importance of acknowledging that too.

Otherwise these will continue with us as 'traces' on our lives and go on plaguing us in different ways. In this connection he cites the example of war heroes who in later years have found themselves unable to escape the consequences of their having killed people, however right it may have seemed at the time: 'The very deeds for which they are publicly acclaimed are the source of confusion and agony within themselves, and this is made all the worse because the acclaim almost inevitably blinds them and prevents them from recognizing the true source of their disturbance'.[20]

It cannot be stated too often how important this is. Confession is about acknowledging our sin, about bringing it out into the open with all the shame and humiliation that goes with that, in order quite simply that we may be forgiven. There is nothing unhealthy about this, in fact it is sin that is glossed over and unacknowledged which produces unhealthy effects. And the priest is there when confession is made sacramentally in order to help us do this. He may also help with advice of course, and more importantly he may help us to see ourselves a little as God sees us. But his main purpose is to make sure that our confession is thorough and real – as real as if we were confessing to our Lord present in the flesh. It was the German pastor, Dietrich Bonhoeffer, who many years ago described this central purpose of confession in a way which to my mind has never been bettered:

In confession a man breaks through to certainty. Why is it that it is often easier for us to confess our sins to God than to a brother? God is holy and sinless, He is a just judge of evil and the enemy of all disobedience ... We must ask ourselves whether we have not often been deceiving ourselves with our confession of sin to God, whether we have not rather been confessing our sins to ourselves and also granting ourselves absolution ... Who can give us the certainty that, in the confession and the forgiveness of our sins, we are not dealing with ourselves but with the living God? God gives us this certainty through our brother. Our brother breaks the circle of self-deception.

A man who confesses his sins in the presence of a brother knows that he is no longer alone with himself; he experiences the presence of God in the reality of the other person.[21]

Of course confession, like everything else can be misused. I have heard confessions in which nothing that really mattered was given away, and when I began to probe gently, the person concerned quickly moved on to someone else! Equally the dynamics of confession and absolution can be experienced quite outside the normal sacramental structure. The small group is one example where individuals frequently experience a sense of forgiveness through sharing with friends matters which are on their conscience. Likewise many authority figures find themselves acting as the recipients of confessions. 'What you have come for is not advice, but *absolution!*' – so a doctor friend of mine to a woman who had come to him to ask about an abortion. And of course any major spiritual experience, particularly if it releases strong emotions, can also be an experience of forgiveness and inner healing. One man described how at a weekend away, in which the church to which he belonged experienced the 'Toronto blessing', he was able to throw off the legacy of his father's brutality which was damaging both his health and his marriage:

I keeled over onto the chairs ... [and] saw myself as a little boy standing by a window, waiting for Dad to come home. The feelings of hope and despair were just as real to me then as they had been all those years ago. At this point, one of the elders put his arms round me. He had been at the other end of the room when he heard God tell him to come to me and to 'put his arms around me as a father would a son' ... Since then the chains have fallen off. I am becoming more sure of myself as a husband in the fullest sense of the word ... Whatever we call it – 'Toronto blessing' or anything else – I know that Jesus through the Holy Spirit touched me with his powerful healing love that night.[22]

This particular account is a reminder of how deep and intractable some experiences connected with sin and guilt can be. Individuals need help in order to acknowledge the source of their trouble – sometimes professional help, often as in this case something other than *words* – some gesture or some new relationship which touches something deep within them. Child abuse is one such area where this is particularly true. The fact that it is now openly talked about is something to be thankful for, but it has also made people aware of how serious the damage can be. Dr David McDonald, the Medical Chairman of the Christian Deliverance Study Group writes about helping those who have been abused, and in particular helping them to forgive those who have wronged them:

In the kind of cases we have been considering, there is immense pain and suffering ... What that person needs is gentle deliverance from the guilt and self-blame, from the belief in that terrible message which was implanted as a seed of self-hatred. There is anger and hate to be expressed. There is loss to be grieved – the betrayal of innocence and trust, the violation of body and mind, the robbing of those birthright gifts of a childhood in God. When all this is faced and worked through, and only then, the sufferer can put blame and responsibility where they belong, and can renounce all the vengeance which has been carried inside. Then and only then is forgiveness complete. But it needs to be worked through with someone who loves even the unlovable. That someone is God. Thanks be to him![23]

It is the experience of most people who are involved in the ministry of healing that healing and forgiveness often have to go hand in hand. Sin and sickness are not two quite separate things; they shade into each other. Where, for example, do you draw the boundaries between sin and sickness in the example we have just been given of someone who has been sexually abused as a child? Or even more obviously with someone suffering from an addiction? In both cases feelings of guilt and possibly anger and resentment are likely to be inextricably mixed with a sense of helplessness – a sense that the person concerned needs to be cured as well as forgiven. So there is no set pattern when it comes to healing and forgiveness. Sometimes it is a confession or counselling that enables a person to be ready to receive the ministry of healing. Sometimes the process is reversed and it is the laying on of hands or anointing which brings about a healing confession. Those involved in this ministry frequently find that healing is a 'two stage' process – an initial ministry which results in 'inner healing' and only then any kind of physical cure. This is something that should not surprise us. After all, as we have seen time and time again in our thinking about this ministry, we ourselves are not in watertight compartments. We should not therefore expect the boundaries between healing and forgiveness to be clearly defined either.

This chapter began with AIDS and has ended with child abuse. Both in their different ways are extreme examples of the way in which sin and sickness are linked. But both also in their different ways raise more questions about this link than they supply answers. As we have seen there is rarely a straightforward equation between sin and sickness, and even more rarely a straightforward equation between *blame* and sickness in the sense that the person concerned has only got what they deserved. Both too lead us on to a consideration of the deepest question of all – what sort of God is there behind all this? That couple's lapel badge with 'My God is not like that' on it, was not only a protest against a particular judgemental attitude. It pointed to the only way of even beginning to know that we are on the right road over this matter. 'God is as he is in Jesus', in Bishop David Jenkins' famous phrase,[24] and that must be our bottom line as Christians, the 'framework of meaning' by which all attitudes are tested. In this chapter we have tried to unpack some of what such a belief means in terms of the deep theological questions. We have also looked at what it implies in practical terms, in how we actually help people through our ministries of healing and forgiveness. But in the end what matters is that behind all our questionings, all our efforts to come to terms with what we are and the scars that life has left upon us, and all our attempts to help others through their pain, the God who is revealed in Jesus is a God who cares about us without qualification and one who wants the best for us – for all of us.

7 Deliver Us From Evil

Evil spirits and the deliverance ministry

There are two equal and opposite errors into which our race
can fall about devils. One is to disbelieve in their existence.
The other is to believe, and to feel an excessive and
unhealthy interest in them. They themselves are equally
pleased by both errors.

(C. S. Lewis, Screwtape Letters)[1]

IT WAS DURING the course of a day long parish visit that the
vicar said to me: 'I would like you to meet one of my
"prayer warriors".' At first I thought he was just using
picturesque language, and certainly the little old lady who
answered the door hardly lived up to that description –
'prayer', yes; but *'warrior'*!? However by the end of the day I
realized that he was in deadly earnest. Here was someone who
genuinely believed that everything that was happening around
him was part of some great cosmic battle between the forces of
good and evil. And he had geared his entire parish strategy to
this.

Belief in evil spirits, the deliverance ministry and the
concept of spiritual warfare have staged a major comeback in
certain parts of the Church over the past decade or so. This has
been greeted with enthusiasm in some quarters and with the
gravest suspicion and hostility in others. In fact it is true to say
that in many ways it is the biggest 'hot-potato' in the healing
scene at the present moment. Certainly those in authority have
been quick to react. Every diocese now has its regulations on
exorcism – usually restricting the practice to recognized

diocesan 'experts', and with the strongest prohibitions against any sort of publicity or unauthorized practice; and there is a nationwide network of advisers, whom bishops and others can consult when need arises. On the other hand there is strong pressure from many clergy and ministers, particularly from within the Charismatic Movement, to be allowed to exercise 'deliverance' as part of their normal ministry. And this in its turn is fuelled by a number of healing centres which are outside the control of Church authorities, Anglican or otherwise, and which teach and practise this ministry extensively. All of which provides a 'headache' for those in authority, which many feel they could do without!

What lies behind this 'comeback'? One obvious answer is that it is part of the general revival of the healing ministry, and especially as it is practised in some Charismatic circles. Certain sections of the Charismatic Movement have gone strongly down this road in their approach to healing, and with this Movement occupying the 'high ground' in the healing scene, it is natural that it should come into prominence. If you delve deeper and ask what prompted this in the first place, you sooner or later come across two determining factors. The first is a readiness to take the New Testament at its face value, and in particular to accept uncritically all that it seems to say about the link between evil spirits and sickness. 'From data both within and outside the New Testament there is no doubt that Jesus was an exorcist – a very successful exorcist'. So writes Graham Twelftree, and on the face of it it is difficult to disagree with him.[2] Then, secondly, there is the suggestion, already noted in Chapter 5, that the Charismatic experience itself could have something to do with it. If this experience does actually awaken the psychic side in individuals, then it is likely that it will make them not only more aware of the power of the Holy Spirit, but also more aware of the dark side of things – of evil at a supernatural level. Dr Martin Israel writes: 'The more psychically aware one becomes in one's own life, the less difficult does it become to believe the scriptural evidence in its own right without needing to accept a fundamentalist bias'.[3]

It need hardly be said that such an approach flies in the face of the prevailing culture of our Western world. Morton Kelsey describes the mindset of the average Westerner very clearly when he says that it is one which 'insists that we have outgrown any such way of getting knowledge'.[4] To the average Westerner reality is what we can measure, what we can view objectively, what we can know through our five senses. Everything else is subjective, unknowable in any concrete sense, and therefore unreliable. 'Our consciousness gives us only the ability to experience the physical world and to reason about it.'[5]

Most of us are to a greater or lesser degree conditioned by this culture, in spite of our Christian beliefs. This to my mind explains why talk about the demonic often seems so alien to Church people, and why it tends to be viewed with such suspicion. While we may well have found room for God in our scientific world view, the suggestion that there is a supernatural realm inhabited by angels and demons strikes us as being so foreign to our normal way of thinking that our natural reaction is to reject it. It is only perhaps when some inexplicable happening comes our way that we begin to think that there might after all be something in it – or if we find ourselves working in a different culture, as many missionary priests and doctors have done. Simon Barrington-Ward, the former Bishop of Coventry, writes:

I shall never forget the impact which living and working and ministering in a flat in a Nigerian Student Hostel at Ibadan University, and spending my first holiday there in a Nigerian village, had on my approach to combatting evil. I had to learn new ways of praying, preaching and teaching. Having travelled since in Africa and Asia and having stayed with people in the churches there, I have realized what a significant learning experience that was. The sense of the powers of evil at work in the daily detail of life is common to so many cultures outside our own.[6]

None of this of course answers the basic question as to which view is right, but it is a reminder that there is a whole area of experience with which our Western world is largely unfamiliar, and which the Church in its turn has for too long ignored or dismissed out of hand. Once again we owe it to the Charismatic Movement for drawing our attention to this. And they have done so at a time when we need this kind of reminder. As has already been said, our culture is changing and there is a growing movement within it which rejects the materialism of its world view, and is looking to alternative spiritualities to give meaning to life. In particular there has been a marked growth in occult practices in recent years, especially amongst the young, and a general fascination with this and other allied activities. If the Church is to cope with this, and in particular with the casualties which are already arising from it, then it needs to be properly equipped to do so. Part of that will mean coming to terms with what is for many a new area of experience and trying to understand what it is about.

Has the Charismatic Movement gone 'over the top' in its concern about the demonic? That is certainly a popular perception amongst critics of the Movement, but as so often the answer is more mixed. There are many in the Charismatic Movement who have a balanced and restrained approach to the whole subject of deliverance and who are only too aware of the dangers that can accompany this ministry. As Bishop Dominic Walker, who is co-chairman of the Christian Deliverance Study Group, puts it in the most recent edition of their book *Deliverance*:

Members of the Christian Deliverance Study Group recognize the valuable contribution the charismatic movement has made to the life of the Church, not least in taking seriously the question of evil and recognizing the place of deliverance ministry in the life of the Church. The vast majority of charismatic churches are aware of the danger of confusing demonic attack with psychological problems or psychiatric illness, and exercise the gifts of discernment and wisdom in deciding how best to approach each case.[7]

There are however unmistakable danger signals, particularly from amongst groups which are not answerable to any sort of Church authority. Bishop Dominic Walker goes on to list some of the concerns which the Christian Deliverance Study Group has, and give some case histories of some of the 'casualties' that they have had to deal with. In particular he instances a number of healing centres which seem to diagnose people as being possessed by evil spirits almost as a matter of course. 'Casualties from these centres will frequently describe cult-like features – love-bombing (i.e. an overenthusiastic welcome), lack of privacy with dormitory accommodation, lack of sleep, idolizing of the leader and teaching which cannot be questioned without being accused of being in league with the devil.'[8] Then there are centres which offer weekend courses in deliverance, with the implication that once you have attended one of these you are qualified to exercise this ministry. And there are some more bizarre features as well: 'A common feature is to view spirits as if they have a physical as well as spiritual properties, claiming that they invade people through bodily orifices and that they have to be expelled through their point of entry'.[9]

There is too a tendency amongst many of these groups to see devils lurking round almost every corner. I myself have seen a list from a healing centre which majored on the 'demonic', which warned its supporters against a whole string of practices which might well be 'cover' for evil spirits 'counterfeiting' as good. Yoga, acupuncture, and homoeopathic medicine were included, along of course with ouija boards, tarot cards and the like. This was perhaps predictable, though not everyone would agree that all forms of alternative medicine have an occult base and were therefore an 'entry point' for the demonic. But the leaflet went on to list other danger points through which evil spirits might get in on the act, which many people certainly would not see in that way – addictions, sexual sins, strong personal attachments, and even contact with a dead body. 'Satan can also counterfeit the "Laying on of Hands" so beware touch (even perhaps an anaesthetist laying on hands when unconscious!).'[10]

Most people feel instinctively that there is something unhealthy about this kind of thing, and certainly the feelings of paranoia and fear which it so often induces would seem to bear this out. But it is one thing to say that; it is quite another to tackle the theological and other issues that underlie it. After all, this is in some ways a very New Testament way of looking at things. First-century Judaism had a well-developed demonology, and it was from this background that the Gospels sprang. Indeed it was Jesus' background too, and it is clear from the Gospels that he shared many of his contemporaries' beliefs on these matters. What then are we to think of this, and what is the real truth about evil spirits and the need for a deliverance ministry?

In the New Testament, and particularly in the first three Gospels, we find that the writers portray Jesus' ministry very much in terms of a battle against evil. As N. T. Wright has written in his recent book, *Jesus and the Victory of God*:

[His 'mighty works'] appear to be a vital part of what Jesus describes as the breaking-in of the kingdom, not least in terms of the battle with the satan, the accuser. Thus the exorcisms, in particular, are not simply the release from strange bondage of a few poor benighted souls. (Nor are they all to be explained away with a rationalistic reductionism.) For Jesus and the evangelists, they signalled something far deeper that was going on, namely, the real battle of the ministry, which was not a round of fierce debates with the keepers of orthodoxy, but head-on war with the satan. This belief made perfect sense within the first-century Jewish worldview that Jesus shared.[11]

The question is, of course, are we bound to share that world view as well? Because Jesus saw things this way, do we have to? Some would answer 'yes' without any hesitation and not only would accept Jesus' diagnosis of illnesses such as schizophrenia as being demonic in origin, but would also accept the whole scenario of cosmic warfare which seems to lie behind his proclamation of the 'Kingdom'. Others would be more cautious, especially over the matter of what causes mental illness, but would still want to cite Jesus' practice as evidence for the existence of evil spirits. Yet others would wish to 'demythologize' the whole thing, and say that, while it would be natural for Jesus to act in this way as a man of his own time, we start from a very different body of knowledge both about the world and about illness in particular.

This takes us straight into the classical Christological question as to whether our Lord's knowledge was limited, and if so how far. There have been times in the Church's history when Jesus has been portrayed as a sort of divine figure even in his humanness – possessing supernatural knowledge, performing miracles, totally in control of events. Today the emphasis is all the other way, on Jesus being a human being like us, limited in his knowledge, and with a full range of human passions and weaknesses. Indeed, it is argued, if he were not, then it cannot be said that God really became a human being in the full sense, that there was a real 'incarnation'. This is an old argument which, in spite of its modern appearance, goes back to the earliest days of the controversies over the nature of the Godhead and of Christ's Person in the fourth and fifth centuries. It is encapsulated in the famous phrase of St Gregory of Nazianzus: 'What has not been assumed has not been healed'.[12] However it must be said that many modern interpretations of what it means to be 'fully human' go a great deal further than the Early Fathers would ever have been prepared to go. The tendency was always to see Jesus as a 'semi-divine' being, whereas the tendency now is very much the opposite and can quickly turn into rejecting the idea of Jesus being 'divine' in any meaningful sense at all.

For my own part I see no problem in accepting the suggestion that Jesus' knowledge of such things as the origin of the universe or the causes of disease was limited by what was known about such things in the first century AD. I would imagine that along with most of his contemporaries he believed that the earth was flat and that heaven existed as a place 'above the bright blue sky'. In fact I would find it much more of a problem if I thought that he actually knew the answers to these matters, but concealed the fact from his contemporaries. That is moving dangerously close to the 'docetic' Christ,[13] whose whole ministry was a sort of charade. So I certainly believe that at one level at least we are not bound to accept, for example, his diagnosis of what appears to be epilepsy, in the account in Mark chapter 9, as being due to an evil spirit. And the same would go for his approach to mental illness in general.

However I say 'at one level at least' because there is rather more to this than just the matter of surface diagnosis. It has been common in debates about the limitations to our Lord's knowledge to make a distinction between his factual knowledge and his *intuition*. It is his religious intuition – the intuition of One who was perfectly united with his heavenly Father – that gives his teaching and insights a unique authority. So some would argue, for example, that while we should treat with the utmost seriousness his insights into disease as being part of the disorder of creation and having no place in God's Kingdom, at the same time we are free to question the first-century forms in which he expressed this. Or again while we must accept his insight about the world being in the grip of 'evil', we do not necessarily have to accept his view that it was in the grip of the 'evil one'. It must be said, however, that this distinction is not as clear cut as is often made out. This is especially so if Jesus' intuition was linked with a strong psychic awareness. This seems more than a possibility – certainly the experience of others who are close to God would suggest that this is a common accompaniment of holiness – in which case 'evil' would be likely to present itself to him under the guise of 'spirits' or something similar, regardless of his first-century background. So we certainly need to be cautious about writing off any idea of evil spirits altogether, just as we need to be equally cautious about using the New Testament as a medical textbook. As so often with things to do with the ministry of healing, there is no one straightforward answer.

I suppose there will always be differences of opinion as to whether evil spirits actually exist as real entities as opposed to being simply personifications of evil. Here I am indebted to the writer, Susan Howatch, for some particularly illuminating thoughts on the whole matter. In one of her books she describes a scene in which the psychic ordinand Nicholas exorcises a demon from a man who is threatening his life. At the same time the girl who is with him strikes the man down with the cross from the altar. When her father, a priest who specializes in deliverance, appears on the scene, they each give their account of what happened. Rachel's is totally matter of fact. On the other hand Nicholas claims to have seen the demon splitting asunder with black blood and a stench of sulphur. To Rachel this is utter rubbish, but to Nicholas it is very real indeed. Later, when he asks her father who was right, the priest says:

It was real, it happened. It worked. You called on the greatest exorcist of all time and aligned yourself with his power. On one level of reality Rachel was given the chance to strike the physical blow, and on another level of reality you were given the chance to strike the spiritual blow. Rachel saw Perry die and you saw the demon split apart in a shower of black blood, but what you both saw with your different eyes was the Dark receding before the Light.[14]

And he concludes: 'Remember that her blindness is God's gift to her, just as your sight is God's gift to you.'

I find this extraordinarily helpful, especially as someone who is not particularly psychic but who from time to time associates with people who definitely are. We see the same reality, but we see it with different eyes. So for some evil will take on the form of hostile entities, and they will use the term 'evil spirits' freely to describe what they experience. For others, if they speak of 'evil spirits' at all, it will be to use the phrase as a 'model' – a way of describing those external pressures and deep internal fears which afflict individuals and which sometimes manifest themselves in bizarre and disturbing ways. This of course says nothing about whether such things as evil spirits actually exist, let alone whether they are created beings of pure spirit, fallen angels, as tradition has it. It is certainly possible that they do exist, and our Lord obviously believed that they did. But other explanations are also possible, for example that they represent particularly powerful manifestations of the evil which is endemic in our society or unhealed areas of our unconscious mind. I am reminded of Sister Wendy Beckett's delightful description of an angel as 'the tender Presence of the Holy One, made visible in the angel, God is present as all-encompassing Love'.[15] Talk of 'evil spirits' could be the 'making visible' of a sense of the presence of evil within and around us, which can in some instances be so powerful as to feel like 'demonic oppression', or even 'possession'. In this connection too, it needs to be remembered how susceptible we actually are, and how no human being is truly an 'island'. We still know very little about how our minds work in relation to other people's minds, but it is very clear that there are other levels through which we can be 'got at' besides that of rational persuasion. Christopher Bryant speaks of the way that 'everywhere mind flows into mind' and how 'individuals are unconsciously linked together'. 'Like islands of an archipelago, joined together underneath the sea that separates them, we are knit together by invisible and unconscious ties.'[16]

So it is possible to keep an open mind about whether such things as evil spirits actually exist, though for my own part, if I were pressed, I think I would be prepared to put my money on the fact that they do. But notice, this is not an argument about 'objective' and 'subjective'. Evil is all too objective, whether felt as external pressures and internal fears or personalized as 'evil spirits'. It was one of Jung's complaints that

Christian theologians did not take evil seriously enough, and this needs to be taken on board.[17] Evil is all too real, and to underestimate its power to harm and even destroy individuals is the height of foolishness.

What then of those who see evil spirits round every corner? As I said earlier most of us feel instinctively that there is something unhealthy about this, especially when it leads to feelings of fear and paranoia. Dr Andrew Walker, the Director of the C. S. Lewis Centre, who has thoroughly researched this aspect of the deliverance ministry, gives a vivid description of some of the more extreme positions that it can lead to. In a section headed 'The Paranoid Universe' in a book entitled *The Charismatic Movement, the Search for a Theology*, he writes:

In the paranoid universe, not only can Christians become demonized, but so too can whole social groups. For example, other world religions are not simply different, wrong, in error, or as Lewis would prefer to see it, unfulfilled; they are the agents of devilish control. And homosexuals are not to be seen as exercising a preference, suffering from a sickness, or living in old-fashioned sin: they are under demonic thrall ... In the paranoid universe women are particularly prone to persecution, especially if they are feminists. Feminism is under the province of the Spirit of Jezebel ... In the paranoid universe the demons can also reach us indirectly, especially through charms, artefacts, and bracelets ... Belief in the efficacy of witchcraft and curses now seems to be mandatory in many charismatic fellowships. Demonic influence not only extends to amulets ... but it can also invade household ornaments [if] they are types of demon spirits [such as owls and frogs].[18]

One is reminded here of other periods in Church history which have given rise to a similar paranoia – for example the persecution of heretics by the Inquisition and of witches by the Puritans. (Senator McCarthy's pursuit of communist infiltrators in America in the 1950s would be an example from secular history.) Fear is at the root of all forms of paranoia, and this is why normal, balanced people instinctively recoil from it. But it is not just a matter of instinct. In the first place we are assured that in Christ, God has shown himself stronger than the very worst that can happen to us, so that even if you believe that there are devils round every corner, you can still rejoice with those first disciples that in his name 'even the demons submit to us'.[19] And then of course there is the powerful fact, which is so central to the gospel, that our Lord's way was to meet hatred with love. It is the fact that these groups seem so often to move on from fear to the persecution of those whom they demonize that makes them so suspect. This is not the gospel as we have received it, and we should not in any way be swayed by the fear and hatred which lies at the root of their position. Again to quote Dr Andrew Walker:

It is here that we move to the heart of the problem. Paranoia breeds fear. Ironically, what is demonic about the paranoid universe is not that it is a world that suddenly sees demons everywhere, but that it is a world in bondage to fear. As evangelist Geoff Crocker reminded me, the Scriptures tell us that 'perfect love casts out fear' (*1 John 4.18*), and yet we find the fellowships that see demons everywhere firstly become fearful, and out of their fear they then become belligerent ... How strange that the heightened experience of persecution which is the hallmark of the paranoid universe is inverted, so that fighting back at your supposed enemies entails persecuting your alleged persecutors. This is what happens when spiritual warfare becomes an attempt to match power with power, meet hate with hate of hate, rather than as Jesus commanded, 'Love your enemies, do good to those who hate you, bless those who curse you, pray for those who ill-treat you' (*Luke 6.27-8*).[20]

Of course not all of those who see demonic activity as widespread would go to the extremes described above. Bishop Graham Dow's Grove booklet entitled *Those Tiresome Intruders* attempts to cut evil spirits down to size by its very title, though in spite of this he very clearly regards them as rather more than just a 'nuisance value'.[21] And his (admittedly 'cautious') chapter on 'Clues to Recognizing the Presence of Evil Spirits' could in the wrong hands lead to the sort of paranoia which Dr Andrew Walker describes. I have certainly heard some very strange arguments in support of the widespread activity of evil spirits. In particular I remember an inverted form of the 'God of gaps' argument being used to demonize acupuncture, something which many doctors now regard as a useful therapy even if they do not understand how it works. The argument went like this: we do not understand how acupuncture works, therefore it must be due to some supernatural force; since it derives from a non-Christian religious source, therefore that force must be demonic; QED! Fear unfortunately breeds its own logic (and its own exegesis of the Scriptures as well!),[22] and for this reason is often unshakeable. But it can lead to some very negative and even dangerous positions.

Catholics are perhaps less susceptible to this kind of thinking, because in general they see things in less black and white terms than Protestants. As has already been said, if Christ is 'the true light which gives light to everyone',[23] then there is room for thinking that many things are good, even if they take place outside the circle of the Christian Faith. So the dualism of theologies like John Wimber's, which sees everything as belonging either to the 'kingdom' of God or of Satan, with these two kingdoms permanently at war with each other, is not likely to hold much appeal. Of course Catholics use the language of 'spiritual warfare' like everyone else, but there is always room in their thinking (or there ought to be) for the idea that some things are 'neutral'. So they will tend to see such things as alternative medicine in this way, rather than as demonic – capable of being used rightly or misused, but in themselves neither good nor bad. And certainly as far as other Faiths are concerned, they are far more likely to see these as fellow movements seeking after the truth rather than as the work of Satan. So George Appleton, who was Archbishop in Jerusalem, could pray that 'men may find in their own religions some clue which shall lead them to see in Christ the goal of their hopes',[24] and this represents the respect for others and their beliefs which is at the heart of all interfaith dialogue. Of course there are some things that Christians should definitely avoid. Involvement with the occult – ouija boards, tarot cards, recourse to fortune tellers and mediums – can result in mental disturbance, particularly in the case of vulnerable individuals. Even if you dismiss the idea that 'something nasty' can get in on the act, the whole notion of wanting to know the future, or (in the case of spiritualism) bring back the past, is clean contrary to the Christian way of walking in daily trust in the love and providence of God. But just because some things are definitely harmful, it does not mean that everything in the non-Christian world is satanic.

Can 'something nasty' get in on the act? The Christian Deliverance Study Group clearly believes that it can, though not nearly as frequently as many people imagine. They quote the old dictum, 'You don't catch demons like you catch a cold',[25] and have a whole chapter in the latest edition of their book on 'Possession Syndrome', that is on states of mind in which people think that they are possessed but in actual fact are not. Included under this heading are certain forms of mental illness, most notably schizophrenia, and a number of 'neurotic and personality disorders'. But they include other situations as well: reactions in bereavement when individuals have dabbled in spiritualism and believe themselves to be subject to attacks by malign spirits as a result; similar reactions following involvement in occult practices; and casualties from Charismatic groups. In the case of mental illness the Group advises that 'no form of exorcism should be attempted. It will be potentially extremely harmful. Medical or psychological treatment is primary, but spiritual counselling and sacramental healing, where appropriate, are a timely contribution to the whole care of the person.' [26]

The Group goes on to identify what it describes as 'a residue of cases where the only remaining diagnosis is the

activity of an evil spirit, and for which the only effective remedy will be that of exorcism'.[27] It sees this activity as taking the
form of a 'spectrum', starting with straightforward *'temptation'*;
moving from there to temptation 'which is so intense that it has
to be described as demonic *obsession'*; from there to *'oppression*
. in which there is occult or demonic attack through dreams or
otherwise; to *'possession'* when 'the person's will is taken over
by an intruding alien entity'.[28] It sees this last as being rare and
only coming about either through direct invitation by the person concerned or through a situation in which they put themselves seriously at risk by involvement in the occult. In all cases
the golden rule is to look for natural explanations first and
work in close conjunction with a medical practitioner. As to
treatment the Christian Deliverance Study Group gives the
following advice:

There are many possible treatments for those who are troubled by
psychic and occult disturbances, or who have been involved in traffic
with demonic powers. Prayer and blessing, the laying-on of hands
and/or anointing may be sufficient, and are always appropriate.
Exorcism may be positively harmful if it is not the right treatment. It
should be reserved for those cases where non-human malevolent
influence is suspected. Human spirits, whether incarnate, earthbound
or departed, should not be exorcized. They need, not banishment to
hell, but loving care and pastoral concern. When a person is disturbed by the attentions of discarnate humans, prayer, blessing and
the requiem Eucharist are more appropriate than attempts at banishment ... When exorcism seems to be proper (and such cases will be
rare) there can be a *minor* or a *major* exorcism. Minor exorcisms are
common and can be frequent. The Lord's Prayer itself, with its
petition to 'deliver us from [the] evil [one]', is a minor exorcism, as is
any prayer which contains a general request to be delivered from the
powers of evil. The minor exorcism is a *prayer* to God, while the
major exorcism is a *command* to an unclean spirit. The major exorcism
will be a very rare event and will be preceded by careful investigation, both spiritual and psychological. It should not be carried out on

an individual unless the diocesan bishop has sanctioned it.[29]

The Group concludes: 'Since the bishop is not likely to give his permission unless his adviser or deliverance team has investigated the case on his behalf, it is not necessary to give further advice or instruction in this present publication.'[30] A wise policy – but the Group does give a form for a minor exorcism taken from the 1983 draft report made by the Liturgical Committee of the Province of South Africa. The operative prayer is as follows and may be seen as a model:

Lord God of Hosts, before your presence the armies of hell are put to flight. Deliver *N.* from the assaults and temptations of the evil one. Free *him* from every evil and unclean spirit that may be assailing *him*. Strengthen and protect *him* by the power of your Holy Spirit; through Jesus Christ our Lord. Amen.[31]

For centuries the Church began its night prayer with the warning from Scripture: 'Brethren, be sober, be vigilant; because your adversary the devil, as a roaring lion, walketh about, seeking whom he may devour: whom resist stedfast in the faith.' This is a reminder, if we need one, that the language of spiritual warfare has a long and honoured place in the thinking of the Church. And this is as it should be, because it corresponds to our experience of evil as a reality, whether we believe in the actual existence of evil spirits or not. But the Office of Compline continues with the versicle and response: 'Our help is in the Name of the Lord. Who hath made heaven and earth.' And that is a reminder, if we need one, that in Christ the victory over evil has been won. Traditionally the Church has always taken evil seriously, but it has generally tried also to keep it firmly in its place as a negative aspect of life which pales into insignificance in the face of all the glorious and positive things that the gospel has to say about God's nature and love. Coping with evil is always a matter of proportion, and that is where the teaching of some Christian groups fails the test. The gospel has other things to say which matter much more, and which do not give rise to feelings of fear and paranoia. Ironically the last word on all this could come from 'Screwtape' himself, that senior devil in C. S. Lewis's ever popular *Screwtape Letters*, who in a typical outburst once said of God (or rather 'the Enemy' as he called him):

He's a hedonist at heart. All those fasts and vigils and stakes and crosses are only a facade. Or only like foam on the sea shore. Out at sea, out in His sea, there is pleasure, and more pleasure. He makes no secret of it: at His right hand are 'pleasures for evermore'.[32]

8 Our Sick Society

The wider picture: social aspects of sickness and healing

Health is not primarily medical ... The causes of disease in the world are social, economic and spiritual, as well as bio-medical. Health is most often an issue of justice, of peace, of integrity of creation, and of spirituality.

('Healing and Wholeness', the Report of a Study by the Christian Medical Commission of the World Council of Churches, 1990)[1]

IN 1970 A DOCTOR FRIEND OF MINE left his busy suburban practice to go out to Biafra for three months to help in the aftermath of the war there. It was like going to another world. In Biafra he found himself dealing with ailments that he never came across back home – or hardly ever. *Yaws*, for example, is scarcely a white middle-class disease! On the other hand where were all those people with depression that he found himself constantly dealing with in the UK? As it was he only came across one case of depression the whole time he was in Biafra. And even that was different. The woman in question was afraid that she was infertile and that her husband would take another wife! (In fact she had already had something like twenty children but had now stopped!)

'Health is not primarily medical' says the quote at the head of this chapter, and we need to take this on board if our thoughts on the ministry of healing are not to be hopelessly narrow and one-dimensional. Whether we are talking about yaws and other diseases in the Third World or the depressions and stress-related illnesses with which our Western surgeries are filled, we need to realize that there is more to healing than just tackling the problem at the level of the individual patient. Other issues have to be addressed as well. Society is also 'sick', and God's healing power has to be brought to bear on the wider causes of ill health – social, economic and environmental.

No apology is needed for including such a subject in a book on *Catholic* insights into the ministry of healing. As we saw in the first chapter, Catholic theology is less individualistic than Protestant theology – though that has not stopped Protestants having as fine a record of social work as Catholics when it comes to actually doing it. But the Catholic emphasis on the incarnation does make a difference theologically. Matter 'matters', and therefore such things as poverty and social injustice matter too. And they matter not just because they awaken our compassion for those less fortunate than ourselves. Social factors matter because they form the framework in which we are expected to live our lives, and it is that framework which actually dictates many of our choices. Margaret Thatcher's 'there is no such thing as society, only individual men and women and their families'[2] simply will not do. Social factors not only colour our outlook, but actually place restrictions on our freedom. And this is particularly true for those at the 'bottom of the pile', the powerless in our world, who often find their freedom of choice very severely restricted. 'I am flabby: a baby of the affluent west weaned on a diet of multiple choices'. So wrote a friend of mine who had chosen to share in the life of a Nepali village.[3] And he went on to describe how the people in the village had no such freedom of choice. From before dawn until dusk all their efforts were spent on just surviving. So his 'ministry of healing' was to help them win back some of that freedom by improving their standard of living. This he did first of all by winning their trust. Then, when they were ready, he led them in a community project – in this case raising much needed water from the river by means of simple pumps powered by methane gas made from cow dung!

What then are these 'wider factors' which make for ill health in our world? The quotation from the 1990 Report of the Christian Medical Commission of the World Council of Churches at the head of this chapter identifies four. 'Health', it says, 'is most often an issue of justice, of peace, of integrity of creation, and of spirituality.'

Health as a 'justice' issue takes us straight into a consideration of poverty, which worldwide is generally recognized as the number one cause of disease. This is so obvious as scarcely to need demonstrating.

It is the poor who are most susceptible to the preventable communicable diseases. In many instances they have multiple diseases so that even if one disease is cured, another illness may finally claim the person's life. Children are the most vulnerable group. If malnutrition in early life does not kill them, it will retard their physical and mental growth and development. In Brazil, for example, 6 million of the 10 million mentally ill are children, and 500,000 children die of malnutrition every year. Eighty-five percent of the 450 million people in the world who suffer from disability come from developing countries, which have only 2% of the resources to treat and care for disabilities.[4]

This yawning gap between rich and poor on a world scale and its effects on health is something that most people are aware of, even if they do little about it. What is not generally realized is that there is also a health gap between the privileged and less privileged groups in our Western society. For example, the latest set of statistics, published by the Stationery Office in 1997 as *Health Inequalities*, shows a difference in life expectancy between men in Social Classes I/II (professional/administrative) and those in Social Classes IV/V (semi-skilled/unskilled) of *five years*, with a similar gap of three years for women.[5] What is more this gap appears to be growing. Taken over the long-term (i.e. from the late 1970s) these figures represent a widening of almost a year in each case.[6] The Report also has some important things to say about the relation of unemployment to ill health:

Unemployment carries a risk of premature mortality. Men and women unemployed in 1981 had excess mortality of about 33 per cent over the period 1981-92 . . . Mortality from all major causes was consistently higher than average among unemployed men. Among younger men mortality from injuries and poisonings, including suicide, was particularly high. Unemployed women had high mortality from ischaemic heart disease and injuries and poisonings, including suicide. Neither pre-existing ill health, nor social class, nor marital status (for women) could account for the raised mortality of the unemployed. This lends support to the hypothesis that unemployment has an independent causal effect on mortality.[7]

These are worrying statistics, particularly in a country such as ours, where high quality health care is available for all through the NHS. However those of us who have lived and worked in areas of multiple deprivation know only too well how true this picture is. As the owner of just about the only unvandalized telephone on a Sunderland council estate in the 1960s, I found myself continually acting as a go-between for callers who needed a doctor. It did not take me long to realize how much easier it is to get the best out of the Health Service if you happen to be educated and middle class. It came as no surprise, therefore, when fifteen years later as a member of a Health Authority, I was given the findings of the Black Report to study. This carried the same message in statistical form, and was one of the first scientific studies of this particular phenomenon.[8] As it turned out it proved too much for the government of the day, who virtually suppressed its findings, only allowing around 250 copies to be printed. The authors of the report were forced to find a printer of their own in order to get its contents more widely known. But there is no denying the truth of its findings or of other studies since then. If you happen to belong to one of the less privileged groups in our society, then the chances of you experiencing ill health in one form or another are definitely greater than if you came from a different background.

Health is also a 'peace' issue. Again this is something which scarcely needs demonstrating. The pictures on the television of the refugee camps in Rwanda or wherever the latest conflict is, with their listless children and fearful adults, the swollen bellies and thin legs and flies everywhere, are more than a sufficient reminder of the side effects of war. And that is without the wounding and maiming which is the direct result of violence. Few of us could fail to have been moved by the pictures of limbless children taking their first uncertain steps, watched by the Princess of Wales on her visits to Angola and Bosnia shortly before her death. And anti-personnel mines are only one example from a whole arsenal of technological weapons with an awesome capacity to deal out death and destruction.

Then there are the effects on health of 'lower key' forms of violence – terrorism and the violence practised by oppressive regimes, and of course violent crime. Here again it is not just a matter of the direct effects – the victims of the armalite and the car bomb, the death squads and the prison camps, the muggings and the beating-ups. It is the way in which this kind of violence disrupts normal life, leading both to poverty and to unacceptable levels of fear and stress. Life was just beginning to get back to normal, was the cry in Northern Ireland when the IRA broke their first ceasefire with the Docklands bomb. Business was looking up, firms were beginning to invest there again, and ordinary citizens were able to move about without the harassment of constant searches and road blocks. Northern Ireland pales into insignificance when compared with some other parts of the world, but the lessons are the same, and all the more compelling for being close to home. All forms of violence have their effects on health, and for those who have to live under the threat of violence, whether it is in South America or Ireland or on some forgotten housing estate on the edge of one of our big cities, the results are all too plain.

Then there are the effects of the arms race. The Christian Medical Commission gives the following as an example in its report:

In the Marshall Islands, where 66 atomic bombs were tested, people still suffer from long-term effects of radiation such as thyroid cancer, leukemia, and congenital birth defects. Many had to relocate to safer but much less fruitful habitations as their islands became contaminated. Thus they have become dependent for their survival on outside help, exchanging sovereignty for money. Healthy eating habits have been replaced by the unhealthy consumption of canned and 'junk' food, resulting in higher incidence of obesity, diabetes and hypertension.[9]

The Marshall Islands are a long way from the UK, and the nuclear testing of weapons has been banned for many years, but that does not mean that we are immune from the effects of the arms race in this country. In particular money spent on weapons could be spent much more profitably on other more positive things. It has been said that for the cost of one new United States mobile intercontinental missile, fifty million undernourished children could be fed, 65,000 health care centres established, and 340,000 primary schools built.[10] Those statistics were compiled at the time of the Cold War, but the 'peace dividend', which was promised when it ended, seems scarcely to have materialized as yet, and certainly has had little effect on money allocated to health care either in this country or overseas. It was the Second Vatican Council which condemned the arms race as 'doing great harm to humanity, and . . . an intolerable wrong to the poor'.[11] And this condemnation remains disturbingly true, as do President Eisenhower's words that 'every gun that is made, every warship launched, every rocket fired, signifies, in a final sense, a theft from those who hunger and are not fed, from those who are cold and are not clothed'.[12]

Health is also an issue of 'integrity of creation', that is

to say an environmental issue. Damage to the environment can damage our health, *and* the health of the generations yet to come. This is a very broad category and embraces everything from the 'doomsday scenarios' of global warming to the additives in the food in your supermarket trolley. One of the characteristics of the last twenty years is the way in which we have become increasingly conscious of such issues. They are now built into the programmes of most political parties, and the Earth Summit in Rio de Janeiro in 1992 and more recently the Kyoto Summit are only two of a number of initiatives to move the action onto the international stage. And at the local level every neighbourhood now has its bottle bank and often its health food shop, and green petrol is everywhere on sale. But the dangers from the misuse of the environment are still all too real. The increase in skin cancer due to damage to the ozone layer is just one example of how an industrial product can create health risks, and there are others which are even more obvious. The smog which shrouds so many of our cities under certain conditions is plain for all to see – and breathe! And you don't need to be a trained nutritionist to realize that wholemeal bread is more sustaining than the white processed variety, however much you may prefer the latter.

The trouble is that 'one person's livelihood may be another's pollution',[13] so that conflict is almost inevitable in matters which affect the environment. Proposals to limit environmentally 'unfriendly' products and activities frequently threaten vested interests, and so give rise to powerful lobbies which make their weight felt both nationally and locally. And even when there is no conflict, economic pressures can dictate decisions. It was the cheapness of the reconstituted protein feed which caused farmers to give it to their cattle, unaware of the lurking danger of BSE. Most of us sense that somehow it is 'against nature' to feed cows with the leftovers from the slaughterhouse, but the pellets bore no real resemblance to the original, and anyway farmers could not afford to be 'choosy' in a competitive world. But in the long run it all went wrong, both in terms of financial loss for many farmers, and also tragically for those few unfortunates who contracted the new strain of Creutzfeldt-Jacob Disease. Whatever else may be said about the BSE crisis, it certainly stands as a warning against taking 'short cuts' with nature. Having said that though, one wonders how much this will actually be heeded once things have returned to normal. Multinational companies in particular have a great way of closing their eyes to such things when profits are at stake. I, for one, worry about the new genetically engineered foodstuffs which are beginning to find their way onto our supermarket shelves. 'They' tell us that they are 'perfectly safe'. But are they? In the long term? And if I don't want tomatoes that don't go bad, will I be able to buy the 'undoctored' variety; and above all will they and other similar products be properly labelled so that I can tell what I am buying?

Part of the difficulty of getting people to have a proper concern for the environment is that so many of its effects will not be felt for a generation or two. The year 2050 (so often cited in global warming scenarios) seems a long way off, but in fact it is very soon indeed in the normal time scale of climate change. And if the sea level has really risen by 50 cm in that short time, disaster will have overtaken the low lying areas of Britain long before then. Moreover I suspect that many people in this country, with its pleasant temperate climate, are lulled into a false sense of security by the word 'warming'. After all a temperature rise of between $1.5^{\circ}C$ and $4.5^{\circ}C$ might even be welcome. But of course it will not be like that. One likely scenario is that the increase of icebergs from the melting icecap will divert the Gulf Stream to the south, in which case we will end up with a climate more like that of Labrador than the Mediterranean! The truth is that we do not know exactly what will happen, but the chances are that we are in for a worldwide disaster unless action is taken now. As the Roman Catholic Report *The Common Good* put it: 'Each generation takes the natural environment on loan, and must return it after use in as good or better condition as when it was first borrowed'.[14]

Finally health is a 'spirituality' issue. 'Spirituality' is a broad term, but in general has to do with 'the meaning of things', and with 'values' and 'attitudes to life'. It could be said that much of this book is about the relationship of spirituality to health. However in this chapter we are concerned with how the values and attitudes found in *society* affect health – or rather 'societies', because the different societies world-wide have different sets of values and attitudes.

Again this hardly needs demonstrating. For example the set of values known as 'apartheid' in South Africa led to the black townships with their unsanitary conditions and festering violence. The Nazi ideology of the 'master race' led to the Holocaust, and in our own day the related values of tribalism and nationalism have produced the 'ethnic cleansing' in Central Africa and Bosnia. Add to these the international drugs trade, the legitimate but deadly promotion of such items as baby milk products where there is no clean water, and a whole host of other activities in which the profit motive reigns supreme, and it is very clear how much attitudes and values affect health.

These examples are all very much 'black and white', and that is how it often is on a world scale. When one looks at this country the picture is much more subtle. For example one cannot help feeling that we are now a less caring society than we were twenty years ago, and that people are more openly 'out for what they can get' than they were before. But the actual evidence for this is hard to assess. Britain is certainly a more unequal society than it was before, and that perhaps has something to say about it. As the Benedictine monk, Thomas Cullinan, has written: 'If we idolize wealth, then we create poverty; if we idolize success, we create the inadequate; if we idolize power, we create powerlessness.'[15] During the 1980s the dominant political philosophy deliberately encouraged self reliance and entrepreneurial activity, and this could be the 'flip' side of that. To be fair that philosophy also extolled the old time virtues of service and family values, but in practice the rewards went to those who 'helped themselves'. So the vulnerable and the underprivileged in our society all find themselves in a position of disadvantage over against the rest of us. This has repercussion on most aspects of living including health.

The effect of attitudes and values on health is illustrated very clearly by the Health Service itself. Everyone knows that the NHS is chronically short of money, yet neither of the two main political parties dared grasp the nettle of higher taxes to fund it at the time of the last General Election. Of course politics is 'the art of the possible', but it says something about the kind of society that we are that such a suggestion was considered to be political 'suicide' by both Tories and New Labour at that time. Here is a direct link between how much we care as a society and health. But the NHS also illustrates in a more subtle way how attitudes can affect health. Health care has always been linked with notions of service, and countless numbers of people have benefited from the selflessness and dedication of doctors and nurses and other health workers down the years. Now there is a real danger of these values being eroded. The introduction of the 'internal market' in 1992 as part of a package of reforms designed to make the Health Service more efficient, also introduced an alien culture into the NHS, the culture of competition. Some would argue that this was necessary if resources were to be used to the best advantage for patients, but at another level its effects are more insidious. Doctors and nurses (and it should also be said many managers too), who have always seen their first responsibility as being to their patients, are now being asked to accept and sometimes make decisions which derive from another set of values. This has inevitably led to conflict and demoralization, both within the NHS itself, but also (and in some ways more seriously) within individuals, as they struggle to reconcile these new demands with the traditional values of their profession. It is not a happy situation, and, in spite of the optimistic title of the original white paper Working for Patients, has in some ways had a very different effect.

Given then that, in the words of our original quotation, 'the causes of disease in the world are social, economic and spiritual, as well as bio-medical', what is the Church's role in all this? In what ways can the Church influence and help change society for the better? Or to put it another way, how can we bring God's healing to a 'sick' world?

One traditional answer is by way of 'prophecy'. In modern terms this usually means the issuing of some statement or report which catches the media's eye and makes an impact on public opinion. *Faith in the City* (1985),[16] which was concerned with deprivation in the inner city and in run down housing estates, is the one which perhaps springs most obviously to mind, in that it caused a considerable stir at the time, and led, not only to a highlighting of the problems associated with these areas, but also to action from the Church, if not from the State. But there have been many others, often associated with particular social problems, but sometimes more general. The Roman Catholic report *The Common Good*,[17] for example, which came out just before the 1997 General Election, was one of the latter, and was designed to give Catholics guidance as to the sort of society they should be looking for and so provide them with some sort of measure against which they could judge the promises of each of the political parties.

Prophecy has never been a popular activity. Perhaps anticipating the furore it was likely to cause, the authors of *Faith in the City* wrote:

While many members of the Church of England have generally found it more congenial to express their discipleship by helping individual victims of misfortune or oppression, fewer are willing to rectify injustices in the structures of society. There is a number of reasons for this preference for 'ambulance work'. No-one minds being cast in the role of protector and helper of the weak and powerless: there is no threat here to one's superior position and one's power of free decision. But to be a protagonist of social change may involve challenging those in power and risking the loss of one's own power. Helping a victim or sufferer seldom involves conflict; work-ing for structural change can hardly avoid it.[18]

Faith in the City did indeed cause a furore. It was denounced almost immediately as a 'Marxist' document, as the product of a Church led by left wing, 'trendy' bishops, and as an interference in matters which the Church did not under-stand and which should be left to the 'experts'. In fact it was a very carefully researched document, and moreover backed up by the evidence of professionals in the form of parish priests, who actually lived in the areas concerned, which was more than the 'experts' could boast of. But its crime was that it made quite specific proposals on such matters as housing, poverty, education, and law and order, and this was seen as the Church meddling in politics. 'The Church should stick to souls and sin' was how one politician had reacted to an earlier piece of 'meddling' by the Church,[19] and it represented the reaction of those in government on this occasion too. The Church had no business interfering in this sphere at all. Religion was an entirely private matter, concerned with morals and the family, and Church leaders should keep out of politics.

As was stated earlier, this has never been a Catholic way of looking at things, nor indeed of institutional Christianity in general. Contrary to popular belief it is a com-paratively modern development. Certainly the great reformers of the last century did not feel themselves to be limited in this way. Evangelicals such as William Wilberforce and the Earl of Shaftesbury were never deterred from using political action to achieve the ends which their Christian beliefs dictated. It is only in recent years that religion has been relegated to the pri-vate sphere, and this is undoubtedly one of the consequences of the decline of religion as an institution. As society has become more secular, so religion has been seen more and more as a matter of personal preference, and less as a matter of national concern. Indeed in a secular society the only way that religion can be tolerated is if it does not impose its views on others. Once it begins to do so conflict is inevitable. Yet, as has already been pointed out, the framework of society both limits and shapes our lives. As *Faith in the City* put it: 'Modern social sciences insist that no analysis of the human person is adequate which does not take into account the influence upon that person of language, culture and social conditions'.[20] So Christians will want to work for a society which reflects the sort of values that matter to them, even if it involves conflict. As Cardinal Basil Hume pointed out in his introduction to *The Common Good*:

Religion is always personal, but never just a private affair ... The Gospel imperative to love our neighbour entails not only that we should help those in need, but also address the causes of destitution and poverty. The deepening of the spiritual life must go hand in hand with practical concern for our neighbour, and thus with social action.[21]

Christians can also work for the betterment of society by means of direct action. *Faith in the City* immediately springs to mind again, because it was not content with 'prophecy' alone. It saw itself, in the words of its subtitle, as 'a call for action by Church and Nation'. As far as the Church was concerned the action was focused in the Church Urban Fund, which was partly aimed at the 'better off' parts of the Church in an attempt to awaken them to the problems of the inner city and to get them to do something practical about it. It was brilliantly successful. By 1993 it had given away over 16.5 million pounds in grants to some 700 projects in different parts of the country.[22] Some of these were quite modest – a grant of £20,000 enabled the people of St Edmund's Church in Manchester's Moss Side to refurbish a derelict pub as a 'safe haven' and social club for people of all ages.[23] The Church had itself previously bought the pub with money set aside for the repair of the church roof! Others were more ambitious, often involving the financing of a community worker for a period of years as well as building work. This project on the Hartcliffe estate in Bristol is typical.

Despite its size, Hartcliffe has no bank, no hospital, no launderette or supermarket, no cinema, no leisure or sports centre for young people. According to local people even the Post Office runs out of money and those who have been queueing since 8.30 a.m. for their benefits have to return home empty-handed ... Inevitably people get into debt, experience stress, come into contact with crime. What people need more than anything else is advice.[24]

Accordingly the Church Urban Fund has financed an Advice Centre there with an advice worker, who is himself training volunteers to assist him. Two of these, who were teenage mothers themselves, are helping the many single young parents on the estate. The wide variety of needs, which the Church Urban Fund projects are designed to meet, is impressive too. A project in Southwark, for example, was aimed at helping young offenders find gainful employment or start their own business.[25] Another feature of the Fund has been its ability to generate additional funding for many of its projects. The fact that a project was supported by the Church Urban Fund gave it a particular credibility with local businesses and others. Typically every pound of CUF grant attracted three to five pounds of other funding – sometimes 'matching' funding from Local Authorities or the EEC, sometimes funding from other charities, who recognized the projects as viable because of the careful preparation and vetting required by the Fund.

    A relevant factor in all this has been a changed view of the place of the voluntary sector in social work in recent years. 'Partnership' is now the 'in word' with the Social Services, and much of their work is now being contracted out to organizations such as Age Concern and the Alzheimer's Disease Society. In the 1950s and 1960s the movement was all in the direction of the State taking over voluntary work; now it is the other way round. This opens up new opportunities for the Churches, and also for individual Christians to contribute directly to a more healthy society through particular projects and through voluntary work. Christians have always engaged in voluntary work of course, but the present climate gives this a new impetus. Moreover there is a new appreciation within the statutory services of the very real 'professionalism' of those who work for voluntary organizations, and this in its turn has contributed to this very clear 'upgrading' of the voluntary sector.

In this connection it needs to be remembered that the statutory services themselves also have plenty of Christians working for them. This is something the Churches tend to forget when talking about Christian social work. We do in fact already have lay people 'out there', in the boardrooms, on the shop floor, and in their local communities, and some of them are in key positions to influence decisions. Even if they are not, they can all play their part in the betterment of society by the way they bring their Christian values into their work. The Church has not always been as helpful as it could in supporting such Christians at work. In spite of nearly half a century of industrial mission and all that has been written and spoken on the subject of Christians at work, most congregations still remain irrevocably church-centred in the way they look at things. I can remember how I used to receive a regular apology from one of my congregation in Reading because she felt that she was not able to do much in the way of 'Church' work. In fact she was a leading magistrate and chairman of the Juvenile Bench, and as such engaged almost every day in putting her Christian principles into practice in what was very difficult and demanding work. She might not have had time to distribute parish magazines, but what she was doing was certainly 'Church' work in the broadest sense – contributing to the betterment of society, and in a particularly valuable and costly way. It is of course hard to accept this as anything but a luxury when you are a busy parish priest and short of lay leadership, but when it can be done, and particularly when help and support can be given within the congregation to individuals in their work, then something very important can come from it. I think of Gordon Hopkins' remarkable thirty-year ministry in the shipyard parish of St Luke's Pallion, in Sunderland. Early in his time there he set up a branch of the Christian Workers' Union for his young shipyard workers, modelled on the *Jeunesse Ouvrière Chrétienne* movement in France and Belgium. His influence on many of these young people was long-lasting, and this bore fruit in later years when some of them came to occupy key posts in their trades unions.

Finally Christians can influence society for the better by their 'witness'. By this I mean those actions which speak of a different set of values from those of society in general and which challenge our normal way of looking at things. Here *gestures* are all-important. 'It is better to light a small candle than to curse the darkness!' This is one of the sayings of the Corrymeela Community in Northern Ireland, which has worked tirelessly to break down the barriers between Catholics and Protestants. What this points to is that there are things about Corrymeela which are more important even than the fact that it does actually succeed in breaking down these barriers in some instances. It does do this and sometimes with lasting effect – by, for example, arranging joint holidays for young people from the two opposing communities, so that they discover that those they have been taught to hate are in fact normal young people just like themselves. But what really gives Corrymeela its importance is the fact that what it is doing is so *opposite in spirit* to most of what we read about in connection with Northern Ireland. This is what gives it its power and its ability to change people's thinking – that it can make this imaginative and courageous gesture in the face of the prevailing hatred and pessimism.

Other examples spring to mind. Jean Vanier's l'Arche Communities, for instance, are not just important because they provide better care and a more fulfilling lifestyle for mentally handicapped people. It is what they say about such people, about their value as individuals, about the contribution they can and do make to society, that matters most. Again we are talking about gestures – actions which fly in the face of commonly held perceptions and witness boldly to a different set of values. Jean Vanier himself writes:

We form a new type of family or community where the strong help the weak, and the weak help the strong. And here we touch on the paradox of l'Arche: people with mental handicaps, so limited physically and intellectually, are often more gifted than others when it comes to things of the heart and to relationships. They can lead us to the home of our hearts. Their intellectual handicaps are counterbalanced by a special openness and trust in others ... In our competitive world, which puts so much emphasis on power and strength, they have great difficulty in finding their place; they are losers in every competition. But in their thirst and their gift for friendship and for communion, the weaker people in society can touch and transform the strong, if the strong are prepared to listen to them.[26]

There is another side to this also. L'Arche depends on an almost equal number of helpers living with those who are handicapped in small family houses. To take this on is to go against the trend in our competitive society – deliberately to 'go down the ladder',[27] as opposed to going in for the social climbing and preoccupation with success which are the norm in our Western world. Henri Nouwen, who himself left a lucrative academic post at Harvard to join a l'Arche Community, writes of Jean Vanier's original decision to go down this road:

When Jean decided to take two handicapped men out of a large institution and bring them into his 'ark', he knew he was doing something irreversible. He knew that from that moment on his life would be intimately connected with the lives of these two men. They had no family to which he could send them, nor could he ever return them to the institution from which they came. This was the form of poverty Jean had chosen after much prayer and a long search for a vocation.[28]

It was a form of poverty with a long tradition behind it, and Jean Vanier is only one in a succession of well-known figures who have gone 'down the ladder' in order to identify with the despised and rejected in society. St Francis is the most famous example, but names like Damian the Leper, Charles de Foucauld, and in our own day Mother Teresa of Calcutta readily spring to mind. And the well-known figures are only the tip of the iceberg. 'St Francis, were he in England now, would go to a tramp ward.'[29] This was the thought that inspired Brother Giles in the depression following the first world war, as he wandered from doss-house to doss-house living as the wayfarers did with no security and sharing their hardships. He was one of the first in the Church of England to embrace a Franciscan lifestyle, but he is representative of many others who have sought to follow St Francis in this way, and their influence has been considerable. Charles de Foucauld died without leaving behind a single disciple to carry on his work, but today the Little Brothers and Sisters, who draw their inspiration from his hidden life amongst the Tuaregs in the southern Sahara, are to be found working alongside those who are at the bottom of the jobs ladder, providing a prayerful presence among them in factories, docks, and offices. And Jean Vanier, who had no thought of starting any kind of movement, has seen his original household of three not only grow into a community of nearly 400, but lead to the setting up of over 100 l'Arche communities spread across twenty-six countries in each of the five continents. Such is the power of *gestures* – both to inspire individuals and to change people's ways of looking at things. It is indeed 'better to light a small candle than to curse the darkness'.

What special insights do Catholics bring to the healing of our 'sick' society? Social work, as we have already hinted, is something which is common to most Christian traditions, but is there anything distinctive about the way Catholics approach this? Do they have a specific contribution to make, and if they do, how does it differ, say, from that of the Salvation Army or from a document like *Faith in the City*?

Here we must be careful not to overstate things, because, except with a few contentious issues which often get a great deal of publicity, the differences do not amount to much in practice, though they may actually proceed from quite different theological emphases. For instance, traditionally Evangelicals have tended to see social work as 'pre-evangelism' – preparing the ground for the important task of conversion; whereas Liberals have seen it more as an end in itself – bringing in the 'Kingdom of God' here on earth. Catholic social work, at least within the Roman Catholic Church, has traditionally been governed by 'dogma' – by the Church's doctrinal stance on particular issues, as witnessed to by a whole string of papal encyclicals. These differences some-times surface over individual matters, as, for example, with the Roman Catholic opposition to programmes for population control, or the anti-feminism to be found in some Evangelical and Charismatic circles, where the subordination of wives to their husbands is seen as being ordered by Scripture. These can be serious issues and certainly explode the myth that there is a 'Christian' answer to particular social problems. But in prac-tice and with more general matters, those who are actually doing the social work inevitably find themselves motivated by similar concerns whatever their tradition, and this has its effect on the parent bodies. 'We will become more pro-active in addressing publicly the issues of the day that concern ethics, morality and justice ... We will further sharpen our activities designed to influence those in power on moral, social and jus-tice issues – from the sanctity of life to racial justice.' This is not a quote from a pamphlet from the Liberal wing of the Church, but part of the *Millennium Manifesto* put out by the Evangelical Alliance.[30] And within the Roman Catholic Church the 'Liberation Theology' of Latin America has stood that Church's normal processes on their head. Far from dogma governing social action, with Liberation Theology the first step is always to reflect on the actual situation itself. Only then does it go on to consider how theological insights affect the situation. Indeed it is the avowed intention of Liberation Theology to liberate *theology*! Its stated aim is to make theology something that can really be of service to oppressed and deprived peoples in their struggle for freedom, and to free it from the 'academic captivity' to which theologians have condemned it. As might be expected the Vatican has not been altogether happy with Liberation Theology, but it has also revised some of its earlier hesitations, and the movement has had a profound influence both within and outside the Roman Catholic Church. Here again we see a convergence of approach at the sharp end of social action, made all the more powerful in this case by the commitment of those who are engaged in this struggle.

[Liberation Theology] is a theological movement which has emerged from a continent marked by extreme suffering. In El Salvador, which has produced some of the most formative theological thinkers of the school, nearly 7000 people were assassinated in the first six months of 1980 alone. In a three-year period, a number of priests, including Archbishop Romero, were killed. It is against this background, in which the proclamation of the gospel is a highly dangerous exercise, that Liberation Theology has made its important contribution to the Christian world.[31]

Perhaps the one thing that can be identified as marking Catholic social action out from that of other traditions is what might be described as the 'mystical element' inherent in it. This stems from the characteristically Catholic way of viewing the whole of life as 'sacramental', something which we have already considered in previous chapters – what one writer has described as 'the overflowing presence of incarnation and sacrament ... the specificity, the crudity of a Christology which sees the presence, the humanity, the dying and rising, of Christ in the bodies and spirits of his sisters and brothers in the world today'.[32] Bishop Frank Weston's clarion call to the 1923 Anglo-Catholic Congress gives something of the feel of this:

You cannot claim to worship Jesus in the Tabernacle, if you do not pity Jesus in the slum ... It is folly – it is madness – to suppose that you can worship Jesus in the Sacraments and Jesus on the throne of glory, when you are sweating him in the souls and bodies of his children.[33]

And in our own day Mother Teresa of Calcutta has a similar message:

'During the Mass,' I said, 'you saw that the priest touched the body of Christ with great love and tenderness. When you touch the poor today, you too will be touching the body of Christ. Give them the same love and tenderness.' When they returned several hours later, a new sister came up to me, her face shining with joy. 'I have been touching the body of Christ for three hours', she said. I asked her what she had done. 'Just as we arrived, the sister brought in a man covered with maggots. He had been picked up from a drain. I have been taking care of him. I have been touching Christ. I knew it was him.'[34]

This approach has sometimes been attacked by humanists as demeaning to the individuals concerned, on the grounds that human beings should be loved and cared for for themselves, and not to provide spiritual 'kicks' for the carers. That is, I think, to misunderstand what motivates people like Mother Teresa's sisters. There is no loss of concern for the unfortunates that they pick up from the gutters of Calcutta, only an added sense of their value and the reverence with which they should be treated. 'They have lived like animals,' Mother Teresa is reputed to have said, 'at least they can die like angels.' And: 'I have come more and more to realize that it is being unwanted that is the worst disease that any human being can experience'.[35] That does not sound like a lack of concern for the particular individuals that she and her sisters are caring for. I suspect too that those humanists who engage in caring work are actually themselves motivated by something very similar. They will express it differently – the dignity of what it means to be human perhaps or the value of the individual – but it is one of the things that keeps them going in what is often very costly work. As with Mother Teresa and her sisters, this is not in any sense to belittle what they are doing. On the contrary, it gives their work a special dimension, one which enhances rather than diminishes the quality of their caring.

Mother Teresa, in the television interview with Malcolm Muggeridge which did so much to make her work public, said at one point: 'For all kinds of diseases there are medicines and cures. But for being unwanted, except there are willing hands to serve and there's a loving heart to love, I don't think this terrible disease can ever be cured.'[36] That is to take us right back to where we started, to the observation that 'health is not primarily medical'. Enough has been said in this chapter to show how wide the causes of ill health are, and also how wide a range of activities is needed to combat them. Enough has also been said, I think, to show that this is not something which either medicine or the Church find easy to take on board. For both it generally means stepping outside their own disciplines and venturing into the unknown world of social and political activity. This can be a costly and a painful process, and one in which it is easy to get one's fingers burnt! But as *Faith in the City* pointed out, it is one that must not be shirked. For the God who heals, is also a God who looks for the righting of wrongs, and if the way to a healthier world involves combatting poverty, injustice, violence, the exploitation of the - environment, and other evils, then that is something which also has to be accepted, and indeed welcomed, as part of what it means to engage in a 'ministry of healing'.

9 God Be At My End

Healing in old age, for the dying, and beyond death

Tibetan Buddhists often show astonishment when they come to discover how rarely and irresolutely Westerners, even educated Westerners, meditate upon the fact of death. To them it is amazing that anyone with any claim to enlightenment, or desire for it, should not meditate very realistically, with the utmost concentration, upon the one undeniable certainty about our lives.

(Donald Nicholl, *Holiness*)[1]

THE FRANCISCAN, Brother Ramon, in a little book entitled *Life's Changing Seasons*, begins the section on 'Autumn: the Season of Contemplation' with these words:

In the Hindu tradition, when a man has come through the successive stages of his life, experiencing the phases of human existence in terms of dependence, learning, working, marrying, begetting and seeing his family grow up, he then may hand over his household burdens and concerns to his son, and either alone or with his wife, enter into a more contemplative phase in which, having laid aside worldly anxieties, and detached from the world, prepare himself for his last and greatest journey.[2]

It is helpful sometimes to look at life through the eyes of a different culture, and in no case is this more so than when it comes to old age and death. Having myself retired only a few years ago, I cannot help contrasting the sort of expectations about retirement which are found in our Western society with the approach found in the quotation above. Hindu culture sees old age as a natural stage in life – to be treated as something which exists in its own right, just as all the other stages do. Our Western culture, by contrast, sees it as marginal – the end of a person's productive life and the giving up of whatever status they may have achieved through their career. 'How does it feel to be a nobody?' somebody asked my wife shortly after I had retired! Her reply is not recorded, but that the question could be asked indicates clearly enough how most people see it. Again Hindu culture sees retirement as providing an opportunity to do what is appropriate at that time of life. That is why it values it as a stage in its own right. It sees it as the time of life for 'contemplation', the time when you come to terms with yourself and with the universe of which you are part, and with God however you may conceive him, and when you prepare for eternity. Our Western culture by contrast sees retirement as a problem – something which may even precipitate a crisis – a time when you will not have enough to do, when you may have to face things about yourself, your marriage, the meaning of life, which you have managed to keep at bay through all the busy years that have gone before.

I was fascinated during the run-up to retirement by the things that were said to me. Most of these came in the form of clichés, but clichés are a good indication of what society in general thinks about a particular thing, and these were no exception. In fact I very quickly came to see them as a sort of 'code' for the way in which our Western culture views retirement and old age.

'I expect you will be just as busy after you have retired' – *code* for 'Will you still be a useful member of society?' As has just been pointed out, worth in our Western culture is measured by results. What you achieve is what matters and what gives you your place in society. 'What do you do?' is one of the first things we ask a stranger, and if they confess to being unemployed then there is an embarrassed silence. We find it difficult to handle the idea of just 'being'. Yet what we are and what we become are at least as important as what we do.

'Well, you've certainly earned it' – *code* for 'Now you can please yourself and life will be one long holiday'. Our culture is dedicated to the cult of 'pleasing yourself' and provides plenty of opportunities for people to do this. In particular holidays are seen as times of escape, when people indulge themselves – sometimes in ways which would not be considered socially permissible at other times. The suggestion here is that retirement will be one long holiday from reality, and kept that way with the hobbies and interests that fill one's time. Yet 'space' in life is a priceless gift just because it *does* enable us to come to terms with reality and those who squander it squander something that is very precious.

Then (most sinister of all), 'You look far too young to be retired' – *code* for 'We do not want to think about old age and death'. Ours is a culture in which death is the great unmentionable – to be banished behind hospital screens and disposed of quickly and tastefully at the crematorium. And we like our old people to be 'wonderful', not only for their sakes, but because anything else reminds us of how the story – our story – will one day end, and that does not bear thinking about. Yet death – our death – is the one thing that is absolutely certain in life, and there is a need to face this and the diminishments which may precede it, if this last stage in our journey is to have the depth and tranquillity that it ought to have.

How are we to help people cope with old age in a culture which by and large marginalizes the elderly? Autumn after all is the time of 'fruit bearing', and the autumn of our lives ought to be a time of great positive blessing both for ourselves and for our families. Patsy Gray, aged seven, hit the nail on the head in her description of 'What a Granny is' when she wrote: 'Everybody should have one, especially if you don't have TV because grannies are the only grown-ups who have time.'[3] The elderly have a natural place within the family and the community and when this is recognized old age can be a fulfilling and rewarding experience right across the generations. Part of the Church's prophetic ministry to society ought to be to help people see this and to speak out against 'ageism', as against any other form of discrimination. And individual congregations ought to be presenting society with a vision of what being an 'all age' fellowship can mean. Yet as the Board of Social Responsibility's 1990 report *Ageing* pointed out:

The Church of England has very mixed responses to ageing and to old age in particular. It both idolises and dismisses old people, and this is reflected in the policies it advocates and adopts. For example the Church talks positively about caring but often fails to recognise the burden which this can impose on family members and the resentment which may follow. It also frequently adopts negative attitudes to older people. It is important that the Church begins to recognise and address its own ageism.[4]

There are other difficulties as well when it comes to elderly people finding their natural place in the family. The sheer number of old people is placing an increasing burden on families, and indeed on other sources of care. It is estimated for example that by the year 2026 (the magic year when the 'baby boomers' become senior citizens) the number of people in the United Kingdom over sixty will have increased by 5.3 million, making a total of 17.3 million or 28.3 per cent of the total population.[5] This increase in numbers is compounded by the fact that the natural carers, the families themselves, are often scattered, with sons and daughters living far away and only able to give spasmodic care. Add to that the high incidence of marriage break-up, and the fact that in many places the natural community, which once provided a network of neighbourly care, has virtually ceased to exist, and you can see why care of the elderly has become such a problem in our Western world.

The problem is basically a social one. Modern medicine can do much to enhance an elderly person's quality of life, but it is powerless against such 'dis-eases' as loneliness and despair. Here the Church has an important ministry. Along with other caring agencies it can seek out the lonely and the housebound, and provide a welcoming fellowship in which their loneliness can be relieved. It can also provide spiritual resources through prayer and sacrament, and through faith in a God who will not let us go, however dark and lonely the journey seems. And it can provide practical help in any number of different ways from changing a light bulb to acting as a go-between with the landlord or benefit agency. Here is a real 'ministry of healing' for congregations. And for individual Christians – because often the work is best done not by Churches duplicating what other organizations are already doing well, but by individual Christians giving their own time to those organizations. It hardly needs to be said that it is not particularly 'glamorous' work. Anyone who, like myself, has had anything to do with such organizations as Age Concern, will know how difficult it is to raise funds for work with old people, as compared with, for example, the care of cancer sufferers or sick children. But that simply makes this ministry all the more necessary.

There is one area of this ministry where the Church has some unique insights to offer and that is in the area of spirituality. Anyone who works with old people will be quick to tell you that attitude is all-important when it comes to coping. 'It is how you feel inside that counts' was how an eighty-two year old lady put it as she laughed and joked with a friend of mine who was at that time chaplain of Bethnal Green hospital, where she had already spent five years.[6] He could not help contrasting her with his own mother, who was living in sheltered housing and who through 'fear of falling' had become virtually immobile, 'sitting in a chair, often sleeping, often leaning forward and gazing at the floor as if watching for fish in a pool'.[7] Attitude is important, and Christian spirituality has some important things to say here.

It has often been pointed out that for many people in our Western society retirement comes in two stages, particularly with the trend towards early retirement. There is the active stage when you still have the energy and health to engage in a multitude of activities, and then there is the stage when you 'retire' from retirement, as frailty and loss of faculties begin to take over. A great deal could be said about the active stage, but it is particularly important that it should be seen not just as a continuation of pre-retirement busyness, but rather as providing opportunities for the individual's continuing growth as a person. Brother Ramon sees the autumn of life as the time of 'maturing' like the fruit in the orchards, and cites Jung on the process of 'individuation' by which psychological and emotional maturity is reached:

This is a process involving time, patience, evaluation and integration. It is a natural pilgrimage and everyone is called upon to constant self-knowledge, adjustment and a wisdom that embraces and uses one's natural creative faculties, while realising one's limitations. The way forward is the way of integration, bringing all one's powers together into a personal wholeness in which all aspects of one's character are examined, accepted and cherished. There may be a call to change and transformation involved, but no call to repression or regression, and no hiding from any aspect that is revealed, but rather a facing up to it.[8]

All this has its spiritual counterpart, and the wise Christian will welcome the opportunities which retirement brings for growth in this way.

However it is when our faculties begin to fail or illness strikes that the real test comes. Here as with ill health at any age we tread a knife edge between fighting our condition and the right kind of acceptance. A positive approach to old age and a refusal to be beaten by its limitations can make a very great difference to a person's whole quality of life, and should certainly be encouraged. However there comes a time when certain limitations have to be accepted – to give up driving, for example, or to move into sheltered accommodation. Family and friends need to realize the symbolic nature of these sorts of decisions, and give support to the person concerned as yet another bulwark of their independence is overthrown. However there is a positive side even to this. All the great spiritual writers have much to say about the right kind of acceptance, and in particular of how the stripping of our natural powers can help us to come closer to God and also prepare us for the final stripping at death. Pierre Teilhard de Chardin has a moving prayer in which he sees what he calls our 'diminishment' as being the means of a deeper communion with our Creator:

When the signs of age begin to mark my body (and still more when they touch my mind); when the ill that is to diminish me or carry me off strikes from without or is born within me; when the painful moment comes in which I suddenly awaken to the fact that I am ill or growing old; and above all at that last moment when I feel I am losing hold of myself and am absolutely passive within the hands of the great unknown forces that have formed me; in all those dark moments, O God, grant that I may understand that it is You (provided my faith is strong enough) who are painfully parting the fibres of my being in order to penetrate to the very marrow of my substance and bear me away within Yourself.[9]

It is natural to fight against the loss of independence, and yet there is a sense in which this loss can be a very positive thing. The Western ideal of the totally independent man or woman, relying wholly on their own resources, is not part of the gospel. The gospel teaches us the importance of learning to rely on God, and often it is only in times of loss that this lesson really gets home. Our dependence on others is a kind of sacrament of this. Moreover it teaches the importance of being a 'good receiver' – often a hard lesson to learn; but it is only when we have learnt to be good receivers that the cycle of love – the cycle of giving *and* receiving – is maintained. Some of the more illuminating passages in the Gospels are those in which Jesus is depicted as a 'good receiver'.[10] He knew the value of the generous gesture and was quick to recognize the love that lay behind it – sometimes in the teeth of criticism from others.

But there is more to it than that. W. H. Vanstone in his book *The Stature of Waiting* sees this willingness to be dependent on others as being something that lies deep in the very heart of God himself.[11] He points to that crucial moment in the Gospels when Jesus allowed himself to be handed over to those who had come to arrest him, and how from that moment he exchanged an active role for a passive one. No longer was he in control of his life – his fate was now in the hands of others. Yet it was through this surrender that God was able to save the world. What this says is that we are perhaps nearest to God, not in those moments when we are actively co-operating with him in some sort of creative activity, but when we are passive and helpless and no longer in control of what we do or what is done to us. In the figure of the 'handed over' Jesus a frail elderly person may see something of their own experience mirrored in the heart of God himself. In particular the idea of 'waiting', which goes with the surrender of control of one's life, is very much to the point here. So much of a frail elderly person's time is spent in waiting – for the doctor, the nurse, visitors, someone to move them, make them comfortable, retrieve something out of reach. This waiting is one of the hardest things to bear, but we can take comfort in the fact that it is one which finds a parallel in our Lord's own experience. And behind the 'handed over' Jesus, who waited in those early hours on Good Friday morning while others decided his fate, is to be found that great heart of Love at the centre of our universe, who also must wait on us – to love him in return, or not.

When it comes to the actual business of dying, Catholics have always had for their strengthening the sacraments of the Church. 'Fortified by the rites of Holy Mother Church' is not a phrase which is often seen in obituary notices today, but it expresses that sense of being carried along by the stream, which is so much a part of what being a Catholic means. Traditionally Catholics have prepared for death through the 'last sacraments' – confession and absolution, which sets them right with God; anointing, now seen as a 'healing' sacrament (and there is often much that needs healing during the process of dying); and holy communion, the *viaticum*, the Latin word for 'food for a journey'. For the dying especially, the sacraments bring strength and comfort through their essential 'concreteness' – the fact that they are things that are done and are independent of our own feelings or weakness at the time. And perhaps even more important, through the power of ritual, they help those who are dying to come to terms with their condition and to accept the reality of what is happening to them. We need rituals to help us move on in life, and at no time is this more true than in those days and hours when we draw near to our end – which is also our beginning.

A lot has been written in recent years on ministry to the dying as a result of the hospice movement. This has been one of the most positive developments in spiritual as well as medical care this century and has had a major influence on attitudes to death and dying. The bad old days when doctors and relatives conspired to keep a person in ignorance of their condition have largely gone, and there is a much healthier approach to the whole subject. Death is no longer seen as 'failure', or as one American research paper termed it 'negative patient care outcome'![12] 'Healing the dying' is how Dr Gareth Tuckwell, the Director of the Christian Centre for Medical and Spiritual Care at Burrswood, describes his work with the terminally ill, and hospice care has been summarized as, 'to cure sometimes, to relieve often, to comfort always'.[13] In particular the hospice movement has resulted in a more scientific approach to the process of dying, with the identifying of the different stages and conditions that those who are dying may go through. These can include such things as initial shock, denial of their condition, anger, guilt, questioning, grief and a sense of loss, anxiety, bargaining with God, and eventual acceptance. The place of the carer, as of the priest in all this is first of all to listen, and above all to take seriously all that is said. Only then can the dying person be helped in the way that is most needed. Dr Gareth Tuckwell has some valuable advice to offer here:

We listen with ears, our hearts and open minds. We listen for issues that need resolution, issues that need healing and reconciliation – with people, with God, with themselves. We listen to the pain of parting, of dependence, of practical concern for the family, of hearing God and wondering how to respond – all this needs expression with the confidence that the depth of the agony will be heard and understood. There may be no space for growth until the whirling of the mind is stilled and the fears that encircle and torment are shared and their reality examined. There may be the fear of something unbearable, of deep sleep being mistaken for death, of failing to get help in a hurry, of being a burden, of being rejected in ugliness, of dying alone, of having no say in treatment decisions, of loss of control, of being misunderstood – all these fears can overwhelm and disable the rational mind. Listening reveals unfinished business, incomplete reconciliation, a lack of assurance that the family is ready to cope; hearing and resolving these problems brings release. Listening allows the mind space to untangle thoughts, concerns and relationships. It gives value to the one who feels of no value – it allows an entering into the other's pain. We need our questions heard and understood so much more than we need our questions answered. If we find ourselves in the listening role, we should perhaps resist the temptation to run for the pastor, they have chosen us. It is their truth they are searching for. On listening we discover some Christians are ashamed of their fear. They feel they are letting God and the Church down, and feel guilty. We can encourage them. God gave us a fear of death as part of our equipment for living. It prevents us taking unnecessary risks. He gave it to us – he understands it – he will help us when we are afraid. Listening can reveal a life story to be recorded or written down for posterity. Dying people are not so much dying, as people, men and women living whatever time is left to them with a sense of urgency – they have messages for those they love but sometimes find it too hard to communicate these face to face.[14]

Here is a vision of what 'healing the dying' really can mean. And the Church owes a great debt to the hospice movement for the richness it has brought with insights like these, as well as through its practical experience of caring, to a ministry which has always held a central place in the Church's life.

The ministry of healing does not end with death. There is a ministry to the bereaved, and it would seem too that there is a 'ministry' to those who have died. 'Requiem healing' and the 'healing of the family tree' are now both well established practices, and in their own way link in with the age-long Catholic practice of praying for the dead and of offering the Eucharist on their behalf.

A great deal has been written in recent years on ministry to the bereaved, and 'bereavement counselling' is something that is now widely taught and practised. Its main purpose is to help those who are closest to the person who has died through the different stages of bereavement to an acceptance of the reality of what has happened. These stages are well charted and may be named as 'numbing', 'yearning and searching', 'disorganisation', and 'reorganisation'.[15] In the first stage (*numbing*) the characteristic response is one of shock, disbelief and denial of what has happened. Sooner or later this gives way to a sense of intense and painful awareness (*yearning and searching*), which may well be accompanied by such feelings as anger, bewilderment, and also with many people by 'hallucinations' – hearing a familiar voice, a cough, expecting the person to walk through the door. This distressing period only comes to an end when repeated experiences bring home the reality that the search for the person is in vain. Then follows a period of sadness and depression (*disorganisation*), which is a normal part of grieving and should not be mistaken for 'depression' in the medical sense. Finally, if all goes well, the bereaved person will emerge from all these stages and begin to take up life again (*reorganisation*).

Things go wrong when people get 'stuck' in one of these stages. Keeping a dead child's room as it always was is an example of this – the reality of the child's death has not been faced and accepted. Those who minister to the bereaved have the task of listening to their pain and helping them to face it, and then at the right moment helping them to move on. In this it needs to be recognized that there are certain aspects of the Christian teaching about the life after death, which if wrongly presented can act as a hindrance to this moving on. For instance the suggestion that the dead person is not 'really dead' can give the wrong signals in all sorts of ways. It can make the one who is left feel guilty at the pain and loss that they are feeling – 'If I were a real Christian I wouldn't feel like this'. And it can prevent them from coming to terms with the reality of what has happened. The Christian hope in life after death *is* a deeply comforting doctrine, and should help a person to readjust to their loss in that it gives meaning and hope to the future. But as C. S. Lewis long ago pointed out: 'There is no good applying to Heaven for earthly comfort. Heaven can give heavenly comfort; no other kind.'[16] Yes, we will meet again, and yes, we will know each other within the love of God and be caught up together in that love, and it will be pure joy. But that future hope is not the same joy as having the one we love present here with us still in the flesh. And even the Church's much neglected teaching about 'the communion of saints' – that those we love are present with us whenever we come into God's presence – can only offer 'heavenly' comfort. Yes, we are linked in prayer, and yes, we may even sense their presence, but again it is not the same as if they were with us still. We need to be very careful how we present the Christian hope to those who have suffered the loss of someone they have loved deeply. It can and should be the thing that makes all the difference as to how they face the future, but applied thoughtlessly as a 'bromide' it can have the opposite effect.

A key moment in all this is the funeral service itself. Attention has already been drawn to the importance of 'rites of passage' in helping people move from one stage in life to another, and nowhere is this more important than when someone has died. James Roose-Evans says: 'A ritual is like a door in the wall which leads us into a secret garden.'[17] And with the opening of that door goes its closing as well. The ritual of the funeral service not only marks the passing into the beyond of the person who has died, but his or her separation from those who are left. A ritual also has the power to release emotions and allow the grieving process to take its proper course. Again to quote James Roose-Evans: 'Ritual works on two levels, that of the psychological and that of the spiritual, and sometimes both coincide. A ritual can resolve, at a deeper level than the intellect, some inner conflict, thereby releasing the individual from a psychological block.'[18] One of the most extraordinary happenings of recent times was the reaction of the general public to the death of Princess Diana. The spontaneous rituals which ensued – the masses of flowers, the pictures, the messages, the queues to sign the books of remembrance, the public tears – all witness to the fact that if rituals are lacking or inadequate, then fresh ones have to be invented. Ritual is something to be taken very seriously, and for the Christian priest or minister is an opportunity to do something lasting for those who are bereaved.

Catholics have a rich tradition of ritual to fall back on, which when properly used touches on all the important aspects of death – its reality and the grief of those left behind, reality about the deceased in the form of prayer for them and their need of forgiveness as well as thanksgiving, and reality about the Christian hope focused most clearly in the presence of the risen Lord and 'the whole company of heaven' in the funeral Eucharist. How different from the tasteful (and if possible unemotional) ten minutes in the crematorium! No wonder people look for other ways of expressing their grief – with elaborate flowers, expensive headstones, and increasingly 'do-it-yourself' funerals.

But even with all the richness of the Catholic liturgy a great responsibility still lies with the person leading the funeral service, particularly if the death has been especially tragic or unusual. I shall never forget the pain with which a doctor friend of mine described the funeral of a close friend of his who had committed suicide. The funeral was in the local Roman Catholic Church and the priest who took the service made no mention of the fact of her suicide whatsoever. And yet it was what was uppermost in everybody's mind. To my friend it felt like a betrayal. This is an awesome responsibility for a priest or minister, but it is one which he or she dare not evade. And approached with thought and care and sensitivity it can bring healing and light into even the darkest place. Sister Frances Dominica, the founder of Helen House which was the world's first hospice for children, has written a beautiful little book designed to help parents through those difficult days after their child has died.[19] It is subtitled: *Helping parents to do things their way when their child dies*, and the assumption throughout is that they will play a major part in all the decisions that follow including the funeral service itself. It is an absolute gem of practical wisdom, deep-felt caring, and rich resources in the form of poems, hymns, readings and prayers. Here is someone who really knows about the importance of ritual (both in and out of Church), and in particular of the need to help those most deeply concerned to find the right ritual for the occasion.

'Requiem healing', which was briefly mentioned earlier, is a ministry both to the living and the dead. Russ Parker in the book of that name[20] describes how in 1975 he found himself sharing a platform at a conference on healing with Dr Kenneth McAll, the author of *Healing the Family Tree*.[21] The latter was talking about miscarriages and the way in which parents so often discount the discarded fetus as a real person. And he instanced cases where the children, in being rejected and ignored, had tried to signal their presence to living members of the family, with the result that these often began to feel the same sense of rejection and lostness as the dead child. Russ's wife, Carole, had had two miscarriages, and the two of them had never fully come to terms with their loss. This whole idea came as a revelation to him:

I suddenly realised that the two children lost years earlier through miscarriage were real human beings. I had been trying to push them out of my mind and accept that they were nothing of value. Ken's talks had helped me to understand that no matter how physically incomplete they were, they were made in the image of God just as much as I had been. This meant for me, suddenly and wonderfully, that we had another two children. They had been lost to us but never to God. It occurred to me that they had gone straight to be with the Lord and had in fact been growing up in heaven with their Father, the saints and the angels![22]

Russ goes on to describe how as a Conservative Evangelical all sorts of questionings arose in his mind, but how nevertheless he soon came to realize that here was a form of healing that it was right to explore and to offer to people. Those who have died are after all 'with Christ', and therefore there would seem to be no reason why they should not be reached through him.

Requiem healing has been found to be of help in a variety of situations. It can be used to help those who are bereaved, particularly when there is unfinished business between them and the one who has died, which needs to be resolved. Death is so final, so that feelings of guilt, anger or the sense of being abandoned are intensified by the fact that the person is no longer there and things can no longer be set right. Requiem healing offers a way through this. It can help in other situations too. Dr Kenneth McAll gives a number of instances where a possessive parent or spouse who has died seems still to maintain a hold over those who are left.[23] When this is recognized and brought to Christ in prayer – including prayer for forgiveness for the one who has died – healing can follow. More controversial is his suggestion that the trouble may be further back in the family tree.[24] To some that may seem rather far-fetched, but he would say that there is good evidence for this, and certainly his approach does seem to help people. Then there are the 'forgotten dead' – those whose lives have been lost through miscarriage or abortion.[25] The 'owning' of these and the naming of them, together with any apology that is needed, can be a very liberating experience. A particular instance of this is identical twins, when one has been lost before birth and the other survived. There is a very close bond between twins, and the recognition of the one who died in the womb has been shown to be of importance for the future health of the surviving twin. In some of these situations requiem healing can be seen as being for the dead as well as for the living. In the matter of the 'unquiet dead' this is its main concern. We know very little about the state of life after death, but there is a good deal of evidence that some individuals seem somehow to remain tied to our world, and unable to find the place of rest where they wish to be. Often they make their presence known through 'ghostly' appearances, sometimes seemingly trying to communicate with those to whom they appear. Prayer on their behalf, and in particular a requiem Eucharist for their repose, seems to be the way to release them, and this is usually evidenced by the fact that the sightings of them then cease.[26]

Although requiem healing is in many ways a recent development and one which is largely being promoted in Evangelical circles, Catholic Christians should feel quite at home with it. Prayer for the dead and the thought that the dead continue to pray for us is something that Catholics (and perhaps even more so Orthodox Christians) have always valued very highly. 'Mutual love realized through mutual prayer' is how one writer describes the 'communion of saints', with the Church seen as 'a body whose members depend on one another and support one another.'[27] And he quotes Iulia de Beausobre on how the Orthodox see it: 'The Church ... is to the Russians a meeting-place of men dead, alive and yet to be born, who loving one another, come together round the rock of the Altar to proclaim their love of God in the way prescribed by Him.'[28] That this meeting place can also be a place of healing is something that should not in any way surprise us, for death, as we have seen, can leave many bits of unfinished business behind – both for the living and apparently also for the dead. But in prayer and sacrament, in the presence of their living Lord, the living and the dead can meet again. So the guilt and the fear and the bitterness and whatever else afflicts them can be healed, as they are brought together in the presence of that all-embracing and reconciling love which encompasses both earth and heaven.

Having now reached the end of this book on 'Catholic insights into the ministry of healing', I find it fascinating that the very last example should be one in which a number of Evangelicals have discovered some of those insights for themselves. I am also aware, however, that if I had arranged the chapters differently, it could equally well have been the other way round. For, unless you have a closed mind, the one thing that you quickly discover about the ministry of healing is that it steadfastly refuses to be tied down to any one theological system. As was said at the beginning, it is theologically very untidy – like the loose ends and criss-cross threads at the back of a piece of weaving. There is a pattern there, but we can only dimly perceive it. And it can make a mockery of our own neat and tidy patterns. That is why it is so good to have a part in it. It makes us humble, and in particular it makes us humble because we rightly fear to engage in 'armchair theology' in the presence of another's pain. But it also makes us expectant, for it has the capacity to surprise us. And again 'armchair theology' is out, because the surprises are real and sometimes a challenge to our whole way of looking at life. But that surely is what we should expect, for is that not how God deals with us in every aspect of our lives – sometimes bruising our shins against awkward bits of reality and at other times opening up new vistas through someone we have met or something we have experienced? 'Everything is encounter', says Archbishop Anthony in one of his books on prayer,[29] and this was never more true than in those moments when one looks for healing, either for oneself or for others. In the realities which are so much a part of sickness and healing, we have the opportunity to encounter Reality itself, and that is what makes it at one and the same time such a testing and yet exciting part of our pilgrimage.

Notes

INTRODUCTION

1. Dorothy L. Sayers, *The Man Born to be King* (Victor Gollancz, 1943), p. 214.
2. W. Williams, 'Guide me, O thou great Redeemer', in *Hymns Ancient & Modern Revised*, no. 296, verse 2.
3. Revelation 22:1-2.

CHAPTER 1: A Rich and Varied Pattern

1. George Carey, 'Revitalizing the Catholic Tradition' in *Living Tradition*, edited by Jeffrey John (Darton, Longman & Todd, 1992), p. 19.
2. Gerald Priestland, *The Case Against God*, Programme 5, 'Artists in Evidence'.
3. John 1:14 (Authorized Version).
4. John Betjeman, 'Christmas' in *Church Poems* (Pan Books, 1982), p. 49. Used by kind permission of John Murray (Publishers) Ltd.
5. Esther de Waal, *A World Made Whole* (Fount Paperbacks, 1991), p. 10.
6. *The Daily Office SSF* (Mowbray, 1992), p. 311.
7. Lewis Carroll, *Alice's Adventures in Wonderland* (1865), chapter 3.
8. David Jenkins and Lavinia Byrne, 'Catholicism in the Future. A Dialogue' in *Living the Mystery*, edited by Jeffrey John (Darton, Longman & Todd, 1994), pp. 123, 125.
9. Kenneth Leech, *True God* (Sheldon Press, 1985), p. 384.
10. Rowan Williams, 'Teaching the Truth' in *Living Tradition*, edited by Jeffrey John (Darton, Longman & Todd, 1992), pp. 39-40.
11. John Habgood, *Confessions of a Conservative Liberal* (SPCK, 1988), p. 90. In 1987 a new edition of *Crockford's Clerical Directory* was published, containing a Preface which was highly critical of the Establishment. By tradition anonymous, its authorship was nevertheless traced to Dr Gareth Bennett, who tragically committed suicide as a result. To put the quoted passage in context, the Archbishop was making the point that it 'needs to be recognized that there are weaknesses in contemporary Anglo-Catholicism which makes it hard to see how those who at present feel themselves marginalized can quickly recover a more significant position. This is sad and ironic, because in the long-term the future lies with Catholicism ...'
12. R. Palmer, 'Jesus, these eyes have never seen' in *Hymns Ancient & Modern Revised*, no. 347, verse 2.

13. David Stancliffe, 'Evangelism and Worship' in *Living Evangelism*, edited by Jeffrey John (Darton, Longman & Todd, 1996), p. 26.
14. Donald Nicholl, *Holiness* (Darton, Longman & Todd, 1981), p. 16.
15. Rowan Williams and Philip Sheldrake, 'Catholic Persons: Images of Holiness. A Dialogue' in *Living the Mystery*, edited by Jeffrey John (Darton, Longman & Todd, 1994), pp. 83-4.
16. J. C. Ryle, *Practical Religion* (reprinted 1959 by James Clarke), p. 9.
17. David Gillett, *Trust and Obey* (Darton, Longman & Todd, 1993), p. 182.
18. Graham Kendrick, 'The Servant King'. Copyright © 1983 Kingsway's Thankyou Music, PO Box 75, Eastbourne, East Sussex, BN23 6NW, UK. Used by kind permission of Kingsway's Thankyou Music.
19. Cited in Martin Jarrett-Kerr, 'Scott Holland: drains and the Incarnation', *The Times*, 5 February 1983.

CHAPTER 2: A Modern Miracle

1. Daniel Callahan, 'Setting Limits: Medical Goals in an Aging Society' (New York: Simon & Schuster, 1987), p. 60, cited by Peter Baelz in 'Some Theological Reflections on Medical Technology' in *Medicine and Religion Together* for March 1996, p. 8.
2. G. Gayle Stephens MD, 'Reflections of a Post-Flexnerian Physician' in Kerr L. White, *The Task of Medicine: Dialogue at Wickenburg* (The Henry J. Kaiser Family Foundation, California, 1988), p. 178.
3. Dorothy Musgrave Arnold, *Dorothy Kerin, Called by Christ to Heal* (Hodder, 1965), p. 14.
4. Cited by Morris Maddocks, *The Christian Healing Ministry* (SPCK, 1981), p. 104.
5. Morton Kelsey, *Healing and Christianity* (SCM, 1973), p. 117, cited by Morris Maddocks, op. cit., p.104.
6. Donald Nicholl, *Holiness* (Darton, Longman & Todd, 1981), p. 48.
7. John Habgood, 'The Church in Society' in *Living Evangelism*, edited by Jeffrey John (Darton, Longman & Todd, 1996), p. 54.
8. David Gillett, *Trust and Obey* (Darton, Longman & Todd, 1993), p. 92.
9. For a full discussion of this see John Bowker, *Is God a Virus? Genes, Culture and Religion* (SPCK, 1995).
10. David Gillett, op. cit., p. 2.
11. Cited in *The Mystery of Salvation: The Story of God's Gift*, A Report by the Doctrine Commission of the General Synod of the Church of England (Church House Publishing, 1995), p.151.
12. James Goldingay, 'Charismatic Spirituality: Some Theological Reflections', *Theology* for May/June 1996, p. 182.
13. See especially *Personal Origins: The Report of a Working Party on Human Fertilisation and Embryology of the Board of Social Responsibility* (CIO Publishing, 1985).

14. Cited in *The Common Good and the Catholic Church's Social Teaching* (The Catholic Bishops' Conference of England and Wales, 1996), p. 17.
15. *Learn About Life: Life Information Pack* (Life Publication, 1986).
16. John Habgood, *Confessions of a Conservative Liberal* (SPCK, 1988), pp. 127-8.
17. Polly Toynbee, *The Independent*, 1 January 1997.
18. C. S. Lewis, *Christian Behaviour* (Geoffrey Bles, 1943), p. 31.
19. Robin Gill, *The Church Times*, 13 September 1996.
20. Cited by Robin Gill, ibid.
21. The Revd Dr Peter Tiplady, 'Healing assessed by NHS' in *Chrism* (Guild of St Raphael quarterly) for Autumn 1996.

CHAPTER 3: Signs and Wonders

1. Francis MacNutt, *Healing* (Ave Maria Press, 1974), p. 333.
2. *The Charismatic Movement in the Church of England* (CIO Publishing, 1981), p. 40.
3. Ibid., p. 34.
4. John Wimber in C. P. Wagner, 'Church Growth: State of the Art' (1989), p. 223, cited by Martin Percy, *Words, Wonders and Power: Understanding Contemporary Christian Fundamentalism and Revivalism* (SPCK, 1996), p. 17.
5. Nigel Wright, 'A Pilgrimage in Renewal' in *Charismatic Renewal: The Search for a Theology* (SPCK, 1993), p. 27.
6. Ibid., p. 28.
7. Martin Percy, op. cit., p. 14.
8. Nigel Wright, 'The Theology and Methodology of "Signs and Wonders" ', cited by Martin Percy, op. cit., p. 76.
9. *The Independent*, 14 September 1993.
10. Ada Hayward, *The Meditations of a Channel of Healing* (privately printed, 1991).
11. Ibid., pp. 17-18.
12. Jennifer Rees Larcombe, 'A Letter to the Editor' in *Healing and Wholeness* for October/December 1995, p. 19.
13. John Polkinghorne, 'Religion in an Age of Science', The Hockerill Lecture for 1992 (Hockerill Educational Foundation, 1992).
14. Professor David Metcalfe, 'Beyond Descartes: A Mechanism for Miracles', given at the Middlesex Hospital, London, 8 May 1996. Extracts from the lecture were printed in *Chrism*, Autumn 1996. 'T cells' are a variety of white blood cell, known as T-lymphocytes. Lymphocytes 'are involved in immunity and can be subdivided into B-lymphocytes, which produce circulating antibodies, and T-lymphocytes, which are primarily responsible for cell-mediated immunity' *(Oxford Concise Medical Dictionary)*.
15. David Metcalfe, *Chrism*, Autumn 1996, p. 5.

16. Ibid., p. 3.
17. Lewis Carroll, *Through the Looking Glass* (1872), chapter 5.
18. Francis McNutt, op. cit., p. 333.
19. Nigel Wright, 'A Pilgrimage in Renewal', p. 29.
20. David E. Jenkins, *God, Miracle and the Church of England* (SCM Press, 1987), p. 29.
21. 2 Corinthians 12:9 (Authorized Version).
22. David E. Jenkins, op. cit., p. 30.
23. Luke 16:31.
24. Dr Peter May, 'My View of the Healing Ministry' in *Healing and Wholeness* for July/September 1995, p. 42.
25. Ibid., p. 43.
26. Mark 6:1-6.
27. Briege McKenna OSC with Henry Libersat, *Miracles Do Happen* (Veritas Publications, 1987), chapter 1.
28. Ibid., p.133.

CHAPTER 4: Ask and You Shall Receive

1. C. S. Lewis, *Prayer: Letters to Malcolm* (Fontana Books, 1966), p.88.
2. Archbishop Anthony Bloom, *Living Prayer* (Libra Books, Darton, Longman & Todd, 1966), p. 115.
3. Sister Wendy Beckett, *The Gaze of Love: Meditations on Art* (Marshall Pickering, 1993), p. 10.
4. Angela Ashwin, 'Sometimes Prayer is Bleeding . . .' in *Chrism* for Winter 1996, p. 6.
5. Melvyn Matthews, *The Hidden Word* (Darton, Longman & Todd, 1993), cited by Angela Ashwin, op. cit., p. 6.
6. Canon John Townroe at a Workshop on Prayer at the Lay Ripon Conference for Carlisle Diocese, 1982.
7. Mother Julian of Norwich, *Revelations of Divine Love*, The Thirteenth Revelation, chapter 27.
8. Dietrich Bonhoeffer, *The Cost of Discipleship* (SCM Press, 1959), chapter 1.
9. Canon John Townroe, Lay Ripon Conference.
10. *The Cloud of Unknowing* (Penguin Books, 1961), p. 60.
11. Jim Wilson, *Go Preach the Kingdom, Heal the sick* (James Clarke, 1962), chapters 13-16.
12. C. G. Jung, *Analytical Psychology: Its Theory and Practice* (The Tavistock Lectures) (New York: Random House, 1970), p. 192.
13. Ibid., pp. 190ff.
14. Morton T. Kelsey, *The Other Side of Silence: A Guide to Christian Meditation* (SPCK, 1977), p. 170.
15. Michael Burden, 'Creating an Inner Room' in *Chrism* for Winter 1996,

p. 8.

16. *The Spiritual Letters of Dom John Chapman* OSB, *Fourth Abbot of Downside* (second edition enlarged), edited with an introductory memoir by Dom Roger Hudleston OSB (Sheed and Ward, 1946), p. 25.

17. See especially, Bruce Duncan, *Pray Your Way: Your Personality and God* (Darton, Longman & Todd, 1993).

18. Jennifer Rees Larcombe, 'Why did God heal me?' in *Healing and Wholeness* for January/March 1991.

19. Francis MacNutt, *Healing* (Ave Maria Press, 1974), Chapter 18.

20. Mark 6:5-6.

21. Dr Frank Lake in his annual lectures at St Boniface College, Warminster, 1963.

22. Thomas Merton, *Saints for Now*, ed. C. B. Luce (New York, 1952), p. 253.

23. Donald Nicholl, *Holiness* (Darton, Longman & Todd, 1981) pp. 145-6.

24. C. S. Lewis, *A Grief Observed* (Faber and Faber, 1961), pp. 42-3.

25. Mark 15:31.

26. Referred to by John V. Taylor, *The Christlike God* (SCM, 1992), p. 250.

27. 1 Corinthians 1:18-25.

28. Philippians 3:10 (Authorized Version).

29. Michael Ramsey in *The Anglican Spirit*, edited by Dale Coleman (SPCK, 1991), cited by David Hutt in *Praying in the Communion of the Saints: Sermons from All Saints' Margaret Street* (Privately printed, 1991), p. i.

30. Hebrews 12:1 (Revised Standard Version).

31. Esther de Waal, *A World Made Whole* (Fount Paperbacks, 1991), p. 11.

32. Revelation 7:9 (Revised Standard Version).

33. W. Walsham How, 'For all the saints who from their labours rest' in *Hymns Ancient and Modern Revised*, no. 527, verse 4.

34. Archbishop Anthony Bloom, op. cit., p. 117.

CHAPTER 5: Thy Touch Has Still Its Ancient Power

1. Betty MacDonald, *The Plague and I* (Hammond, Hammond & Co., 1948), p. 158.

2. Romans 6:1-4.

3. *A New Catechism: Catholic Faith for Adults* (Burns & Oates, 1967), p. 253.

4. C. S. Lewis, *English Literature in the Sixteenth Century* (Oxford, 1954), p. 459. He is writing about Hooker of whom he says: 'Few models of the universe are more filled – one might say drenched – with Deity than his'.

5. Martin Israel, *Precarious Living* (Mowbray, 1982), pp. 133-4.

6. E.g. 'He will regard all the utensils and goods of the monastery as sacred vessels of the altar' (Rule of St Benedict, chapter 31), cited by Esther de Waal, *Living with Contradiction: An Introduction to Benedictine Spirituality* (Canterbury Press, 1997), p. 70.

7. Philip Sheldrake, *Living Between Worlds: Place and Journey in Celtic Spirituality* (Darton, Longman & Todd, 1995), p. 73.

8. George Herbert, 'Prayer' in *The English Poems of George Herbert*, edited by C. A. Patrides (Dent, 1974).

9. Mark Pearson, *Christian Healing: A Practical and Comprehensive Guide* (Hodder & Stoughton, 1995), p. 172. He acknowledges that he owes this thought to the United Methodist leader, Dr Ross Whetstone.

10. 'Yin-yang. The two opposite energies in Chinese thought, from whose interaction and fluctuation the universe and its diverse forms emerge . . . All oppositions can be mapped onto yin and yang, yin representing e.g. the feminine, yielding, receptive, moon, water, clouds, even numbers, and the yang the masculine, hard, active, red, the sun, and odd numbers' (*The Oxford Dictionary of World Religions*, 1997).

11. *Ministry to the Sick: Authorised Alternative Services* (Joint Publishers, 1983), p. 33.

12. John Halliburton, 'Anointing in the Early Church' in *The Oil of Gladness: Anointing in the Christian Tradition*, edited by Martin Dudley and Geoffrey Rowell (SPCK, 1993), p. 77.

13. Luke 10:34.

14. John Halliburton, op. cit., p. 88.

15. St Ephrem, 'H. de Virginitate' 7.6, cited by Sebastion Brock, 'Anointing in the Syriac Tradition' in Dudley and Rowell, op. cit., p. 93.

16. Sebastian Brock, op. cit., p. 96.

17. Mark 1:9-11.

18. Morris Maddocks, *The Christian Healing Ministry* (SPCK, 1981), p. 118.

19. Rebecca Abrams and Hugo Slim, 'The Revival of Oils in Contemporary Culture: Implications for the Sacrament of Anointing' in Dudley and Rowell, op. cit., p.169.

20. Ibid., p. 170.

21. Maureen Palmer, 'The Oil of Gladness for Wholeness: Hospice Ministry and Anointing' in Dudley and Rowell, op. cit., p. 164.

22. Morris Maddocks, op. cit., p. 118.

23. Ibid., p. 120.

24. *The Book of Common Prayer* (1979) of the American Episcopal Church.

25. *Ministry to the Sick*, p. 28.

26. The American Episcopal Church allows a lay person to administer this sacrament in an emergency, the Church of England 1991 order, *Ministry at the Time of Death*, allows a deacon who has been authorized by the bishop to administer this sacrament, and *The Book of Alternative Services of the Church of Canada* (1985) allows a lay person who has been authorized by the bishop to do so.

27. Morris Maddocks, op. cit., p. 113, citing Alexander Schmemann, *The World as Sacrament* (Darton, Longman & Todd, 1966), p. 42.

28. Francis MacNutt, *Healing* (Ave Maria Press, 1974), p. 291.

29. Briege McKenna OSC with Henry Libersat, *Miracles Do Happen* (Veritas

Publications, 1987), p. 66.

30. John Gunstone, *Pentecost Comes to Church: Sacraments and Spiritual Gifts* (Darton, Longman & Todd, 1994), p. 49.

31. John 15:4.

32. Mark 6:56.

33. Bill Kirkpatrick, *Going Forth: A Practical and Spiritual Approach to Dying and Death* (Darton, Longman & Todd, 1997), p. 16.

34. Gretchen Stevens, 'Healing through gentle touch' in *Chrism* for Autumn 1996, p. 8.

35. Ibid., p. 8.

36. H. Twells, 'At even, ere the sun was set' in *Hymns Ancient and Modern Revised*, no. 20, verse 7.

37. John Gunstone, op. cit., chapter 4.

38. Cited by Kenneth Leech, *True God: An Exploration in Spiritual Theology* (Sheldon Press, 1985), p. 199.

39. John Gunstone, op. cit., p. 36.

40. Kenneth Leech, op. cit., p. 200.

41. Briege McKenna OSC with Henry Libersat, op. cit., p. 58.

42. Carter Lindberg, 'Charismatic Renewal and the Lutheran Tradition', a Report for the Lutheran World Federation, cited by Josephine Bax, *The Good Wine: Spiritual Renewal in the Church of England* (Church House Publishing, 1986), p. 80.

43. Stephen Parsons, *Searching for Healing: Making Sense of the Many Paths to Wholeness* (Lion Publishing, 1995), p. 116.

44. Mark Pearson, op. cit., p. 171.

45. Cited in Dudley and Rowell, op. cit., p. 202.

46. Stephen Parsons, op. cit., p. 87.

47. Cited by Josephine Bax, op. cit., p. 76.

48. Martin Israel, *Healing as Sacrament: The Sanctification of the World* (Darton, Longman & Todd, 1984), p. 90.

49. John Gunstone, op. cit., p. 53.

50. Michael Ramsey, Robert E. Terwilliger, A. M. Allchin, *The Charismatic Christ* (Darton, Longman & Todd, 1974), pp. 101-2.

51. 1 Corinthians 12:31-13:13.

52. Carlo Carretto, *Letters from the Desert* (Darton, Longman & Todd, 1972), p. 7.

CHAPTER 6: What Have I Done to Deserve This?

1. Michael Prince, *God's Cop: The Biography of James Anderton* (Frederick Muller, 1988), p. 97.

2. Ibid., p. 98.

3. John Habgood, *Confessions of a Conservative Liberal* (SPCK, 1988), p. 177.

4. The Church Society, *AIDS and the Judgement of God*, cited in *AIDS*, the

Report by the Board for Social Responsibility for the General Synod (1987), p. 6.

5. John Habgood, op. cit., p. 63.

6. Ibid., p. 63.

7. Luke 18:9.

8. *Ad Clerum* from the Bishops in the Diocese of London, April 1987.

9. Anne Long and Sharon Stinson, *Listening to Others, to Myself, to God* (photocopied leaflet for the Acorn Christian Healing Trust).

10. Anne Long, 'Just Listening' in *Medicine and Religion Together* (the Journal of the Medical Forum of the Churches' Council for Health and Healing) for November 1995, p. 15.

11. E. Hall, 'How Cultures Collide: an interview with Edward T. Hall in 'Psychology Today' (June 1976), cited in *Mud and Stars: Report of a Working Party on The Impact of Hospice Experience on the Church's Ministry of Healing* (Sobell Publications, 1991), p. 144.

12. Geoff Holmes, ' "Christian Counselling" – a process of opening up or closing down?' in *Health and Healing* (the Journal for the Churches' Council for Health and Healing) for May 1996, p. 1.

13. Ibid., p. 2.

14. Harry Dean, *Counselling in a Troubled Society* (Quartermaine, 1981), cited by Geoff Holmes, op. cit., p. 1.

15. Kathleen Heasman, 'An Introduction to Pastoral Counselling' (1969), p. 1, cited by Kenneth Leech, *Soul Friend: A Study of Spirituality* (Sheldon Press, 1977), p. 102.

16. Kenneth Leech, op. cit., p.102.

17. Daniel Day Williams, *The Minister and the Cure of Souls* (New York, 1961), pp. 25-6.

18. Michael Ramsey, Robert E. Terwilliger, A. M. Allchin, *The Charismatic Christ* (Darton, Longman & Todd, 1974), p. 45.

19. Donald Nicholl, *Holiness* (Darton, Longman & Todd, 1981), p. 53.

20. Ibid., pp. 51-2.

21. Dietrich Bonhoeffer, *Life Together* (SCM Press, 1954), pp. 105-6.

22. Patrick Gillan, 'One Man's "Toronto Blessing"' in *Healing and Wholeness* for July/September 1995, p. 15.

23. *Deliverance* (Second Edition), edited by Michael Perry (SPCK, 1996), pp. 95-6.

24. Bishop David Jenkins used this phrase on a number of occasions, but see David and Rebecca Jenkins, *Free to Believe* (BBC Books, 1991), the title for Chapter 5 and p. 61.

CHAPTER 7: Deliver Us From Evil

1. C. S. Lewis, *The Screwtape Letters* (Geoffrey Bles, 1942), p. 9.

2. Graham Twelftree, *Christ Triumphant* (Hodder and Stoughton, 1985), p. 86.

3. Martin Israel, *Exorcism: The Removal of Evil Influences* (SPCK, 1997), p. vii.
4. Morton T. Kelsey, *The Other Side of Silence: A Guide to Christian Meditation* (SPCK, 1977), p. 145.
5. Ibid., p. 145.
6. Simon Barrington-Ward, 'Foreword' to Graham Dow, *Those Tiresome Intruders: Sharing Experience in the Ministry of Deliverance* (Grove Books, 1990), p. 3.
7. *Deliverance* (Second Edition), edited by Michael Perry (SPCK, 1996), p. 99.
8. Ibid., p. 99.
9. Ibid., p. 100.
10. From a paper on 'Deliverance' as practised at a nearby healing centre, prepared by a diocesan adviser for his diocesan healing advisory group.
11. N. T. Wright, *Jesus and the Victory of God* (SPCK, 1996), pp. 194-5.
12. Gregory of Nazianzus, Epistle 101.
13. 'Docetism' (from the Greek word for 'I seem') stands for the belief in the early days of the Church (especially amongst the Gnostic heretics) that Christ's humanity and his sufferings were apparent rather than real. In its more extreme forms it was held that he miraculously escaped death e.g. through Judas Iscariot or Simon of Cyrene changing places with him before the crucifixion.
14. Susan Howatch, *Mystical Paths* (Fontana, 1993), p. 518.
15. Sister Wendy Beckett, *The Gaze of Love: Meditations on Art* (Marshall Pickering, 1993), p. 76.
16. Christopher Bryant, *The River Within* (Darton, Longman & Todd, 1978), p. 95.
17. Christopher Bryant, *Jung and the Christian Way* (Darton, Longman & Todd, 1983), p. 73.
18. Andrew Walker, 'The Devil You Think You Know: Demonology and the Charismatic Movement' in *Charismatic Renewal: The Search for a Theology* (SPCK, 1993), pp. 92-3, 95.
19. Luke 10:17.
20. Andrew Walker, op. cit., pp. 93-4, 92.
21. Graham Dow, op. cit.
22. E.g. the 'owls and frogs' in the quotation from Andrew Walker above. A stuffed toy frog and a mobile from which hung some little owl images in a girl's bedroom were seen as the source of her fear when she woke at night. In Deuteronomy 14:7-19 these are classified as 'unclean' creatures, and were therefore assumed to be the types of demon spirits, and the objects were destroyed. It is very clear however that the original purpose of the text was dietary. Andrew Walker, op. cit., pp. 95-6.
23. John 1:9.

24. George Appleton, *One Man's Prayers* (SPCK, 1967), p. 50.
25. *Deliverance* (Second Edition), p.100.
26. Ibid., p. 112.
27. Ibid., p. 118.
28. Ibid., p. 118.
29. Ibid., pp. 133-4.
30. Ibid., p. 134.
31. Ibid., p. 174.
32. C. S. Lewis, op. cit., p. 112.

CHAPTER 8: Our Sick Society

1. *Healing and Wholeness: The Churches' Role in Health*, The Report of a Study by the Christian Medical Commission of the World Council of Churches (Geneva, 1990), p. 1.
2. Cited by Alan Billings, 'What Sort of a Society are we Envisaging Now?' in *Living Tradition*, edited by Jeffrey John (Darton, Longman & Todd, 1992), p. 81.
3. Andrew Bulmer, CMS Link Letter, June 1981.
4. The Christian Medical Commission Report, pp. 24-5.
5. *Health Inequalities: Decennial Supplement*, edited by Frances Drever and Margaret Whitehead (London, The Stationery Office, 1997), p. 73.
6. Ibid., p. 225
7. Ibid., p. 156.
8. P. Townsend and N. Davidson (eds.), *Inequalities in Health: The Black Report (1980)* (Hammondsworth: Penguin, 1982).
9. The Christian Medical Commission Report, p. 25.
10. Ruth Leger Sivard, 'World Military and Social Expenditure 1980' (Campaign Against the Arms Trade, 1980), cited by Kenneth Leech, op. cit., p. 406.
11. *Gaudium et Spes*, 81, cited by Leech, op. cit., p. 406.
12. President Dwight D. Eisenhower, cited in *Disarmament and World Development*, edited by Richard Jolly (Pergamon, 1978), p. 3, cited by Leech, op. cit., p. 406.
13. *Faith in the Countryside*, Report of the Archbishops' Commission on Rural Areas (Churchman Publishing, 1990), p. 35.
14. *The Common Good and the Catholic Church's Social Teaching* (The Catholic Bishops' Conference of England & Wales, 1996), p. 24.
15. Thomas Cullinan OSB, *The Roots of Social Injustice* (Catholic Housing Aid Society, 1973), p. 4, cited by Kenneth Leech, op. cit., p. 412.
16. *Faith in the City: A Call for Action by Church and Nation*, The Report of the Archbishop of Canterbury's Commission on Urban Priority Areas (Church House Publishing, 1985).
17. *The Common Good and the Catholic Church's Social Teaching* (The Catholic

Bishops' Conference of England and Wales, 1996).

18. *Faith in the City*, p. 49.

19. John Stokes MP, cited in the *Church of England Newspaper*, 6 August 1981.

20. *Faith in the City*, p. 50.

21. *The Common Good*, p. 1.

22. *Church Urban Fund Annual Review*, 1983.

23. *Church Urban Fund: A Sign of Hope in the Pub with no Beer*, October 1994.

24. *Stories of Hope: News from the Church Urban Fund*, Autumn 1992.

25. *Church Urban Fund: Project Summary*, New Assembly of Churches (CUF/37/9/111).

26. Jean Vanier, 'L'Arche – A Gift to Society' in *Healing and Wholeness* for May/June 1997, p. 11.

27. 'Both Jean Vanier and Henri Nouwen write eloquently about going "down the ladder" – i.e. the opposite of social climbing towards worldly success – to find God in those less fortunate than ourselves.' Josephine Bax, *Finding God Today: Contemporary Spirituality and the Church* (Darton, Longman & Todd, 1990), p. 4.

28. Henri J. M. Nouwen, *The Road to Daybreak: A Spiritual Journey* (Darton, Longman & Todd, 1989), p. 12.

29. Petà Dunstan, *This Poor Sort: A History of the European Province of the Society of St Francis* (Darton, Longman & Todd, 1997), p. 1.

30. *Church Times*, 17 October 1997.

31. Kenneth Leech, op. cit., p. 419.

32. Ibid., p.287.

33. H. Maynard-Smith, 'Frank: Bishop of Zanzibar' (SPCK, 1926), p. 302, cited by Adrian Hastings, *A History of English Christianity 1920-1985* (William Collins, 1986), p. 174.

34. Cited by Kenneth Leech, op. cit., p. 288.

35. Malcolm Muggeridge, *Something Beautiful for God* (Fontana, 1972), pp. 98-9.

36. Ibid., p. 99.

CHAPTER 9: God Be At My End

1. Donald Nicholl, *Holiness* (Darton, Longman & Todd, 1981), p. 28.

2. Brother Ramon, *Life's Changing Seasons: Christian Growth and Maturity* (Marshall Pickering, 1988), p. 34.

3. Ann Spokes Symonds, *Celebrating Age: An Anthology* (Age Concern England, 1987), p.16, cited by Archbishop Robert Runcie in the House of Lords.

4. *Ageing*, A Report from the Board for Social Responsibility (Church House Publishing, 1990), p. 138.

5. *Fifty plus: population and other projections* (Age Concern England brief-

ing paper, Ref: 1497).

6. Gerald Garbutt, 'Through Fear of Falling: Towards a Christian understanding of ageing' in *Christian* for Autumn 1986, p. 7.

7. Ibid., p. 22.

8. Brother Ramon, op. cit., p. 29.

9. Pierre Teilhard de Chardin, *Le Milieu Divin: An Essay on the Interior Life* (William Collins, 1960), pp. 69-70.

10. E.g. Mark 14:3-9, Luke 7:36-50, John 12:1-8.

11. W. H. Vanstone, *The Stature of Waiting* (Darton, Longman & Todd, 1982) passim, but see especially chapters 2 and 6.

12. Cited by Gareth Tuckwell, 'Healing the Dying' in *Chrism* for Autumn 1997, p. 8.

13. *Mud and Stars: Report of a Working Party on The Impact of Hospice Experience on the Church's Ministry of Healing* (Sobell Publications, 1991), p. 4.

14. Gareth Tuckwell, op. cit., p. 9.

15. John Bowlby, *Attachment and Loss, Vol. 3: Loss: Sadness and Depression* (Hogarth Press, 1980), p. 85, cited by Geoff Walters, *Why Do Christians Find it Hard to Grieve?* (Paternoster Press, 1997), p. 119.

16. C. S. Lewis, *The Four Loves* (Geoffrey Bles, 1960), p. 157.

17. James Roose-Evans, 'Passages of the Soul' (Element Books, 1994), p. 40, cited by Bill Kirkpatrick, *Going Forth: A Practical and Spiritual Approach to Dying and Death* (Darton, Longman & Todd, 1997), p. 48.

18. James Roose-Evans, op. cit., p. 9, cited by Bill Kirkpatrick, op. cit., p. 49.

19. Sister Frances Dominica, *Just My Reflection: Helping parents to do things their way when their child dies* (Darton, Longman & Todd, 1997).

20. Michael Mitton and Russ Parker, *Requiem Healing: A Christian Understanding of the Dead* (Darton, Longman & Todd, 1991).

21. Dr Kenneth McAll, *Healing the Family Tree* (New Edition, Sheldon Press, 1986).

22. Michael Mitton and Russ Parker, op. cit., pp. 7-8.

23. Dr Kenneth McAll, op. cit., chapter 2.

24. Ibid., chapter 2.

25. Michael Mitton and Russ Parker, op. cit., pp. 107-8.

26. *Deliverance* (Second Edition), edited by Michael Perry (SPCK, 1996), chapter 5.

27. Kallistos Ware, 'Death and Life' in *Christian* for Eastertide 1975, p. 368.

28. Iulia de Beausobre, 'Creative Suffering' (1940), cited by Kallistos Ware, op. cit., p. 368.

29. Anthony Bloom and Georges LeFebvre, *Courage to Pray* (Darton, Longman & Todd, 1973), p. 7.

Index